Library Linked Data in the Cloud

OCLC's Experiments with New Models of Resource Description

Synthesis Lectures on the Semantic Web: Theory and Technology

Editors
Ying Ding, *Indiana University*
Paul Groth, *Elsevier Labs*

Founding Editor Emeritus
James Hendler, *Rensselaer Polytechnic Institute*

Synthesis Lectures on the Semantic Web: Theory and Application is edited by Ying Ding of Indiana University and Paul Groth of VU University Amsterdam. Whether you call it the Semantic Web, Linked Data, or Web 3.0, a new generation of Web technologies is offering major advances in the evolution of the World Wide Web. As the first generation of this technology transitions out of the laboratory, new research is exploring how the growing Web of Data will change our world. While topics such as ontology-building and logics remain vital, new areas such as the use of semantics in Web search, the linking and use of open data on the Web, and future applications that will be supported by these technologies are becoming important research areas in their own right. Whether they be scientists, engineers or practitioners, Web users increasingly need to understand not just the new technologies of the Semantic Web, but to understand the principles by which those technologies work, and the best practices for assembling systems that integrate the different languages, resources, and functionalities that will be important in keeping the Web the rapidly expanding, and constantly changing, information space that has changed our lives.
Topics to be included:

- Semantic Web Principles from linked-data to ontology design

- Key Semantic Web technologies and algorithms

- Semantic Search and language technologies

- The Emerging "Web of Data" and its use in industry, government and university applications

- Trust, Social networking and collaboration technologies for the Semantic Web

- The economics of Semantic Web application adoption and use

- Publishing and Science on the Semantic Web

- Semantic Web in health care and life sciences

Library Linked Data in the Cloud: OCLC's Experiments with New Models of Resource Description
Carol Jean Godby, Shenghui Wang, and Jeffrey K. Mixter

www.morganclaypool.com

ISBN: 9781627052191   paperback
ISBN: 9781627052207   ebook

DOI 10.2200/S00620ED1V01Y201412WBE012

A Publication in the Morgan & Claypool Publishers series
SYNTHESIS LECTURES ON THE SEMANTIC WEB: THEORY AND TECHNOLOGY

Lecture #9
Series Editors: Ying Ding, *Indiana University*
               Paul Groth, *Elsevier Labs*
Founding Editor Emeritus: James Hendler, *Rensselaer Polytechnic Institute*
Series ISSN
Print 2160-4711   Electronic 2160-472X

Library Linked Data in the Cloud

OCLC's Experiments with New Models of Resource Description

Carol Jean Godby, Shenghui Wang, and Jeffrey K. Mixter
OCLC Research

SYNTHESIS LECTURES ON THE SEMANTIC WEB: THEORY AND TECHNOLOGY #9

MORGAN & CLAYPOOL PUBLISHERS

ABSTRACT

This book describes OCLC's contributions to the transformation of the Internet from a web of documents to a Web of Data. The new Web is a growing 'cloud' of interconnected resources that identify the things people want to know about when they approach the Internet with an information need.

The linked data architecture has achieved critical mass just as it has become clear that library standards for resource description are nearing obsolescence. Working for the world's largest library cooperative, OCLC researchers have been active participants in the development of next-generation standards for library resource description. By engaging with an international community of library and Web standards experts, they have published some of the most widely used RDF datasets representing library collections and librarianship.

This book focuses on the conceptual and technical challenges involved in publishing linked data derived from traditional library metadata. This transformation is a high priority because most searches for information start not in the library, nor even in a Web-accessible library catalog, but elsewhere on the Internet. Modeling data in a form that the broader Web understands will project the value of libraries into the Digital Information Age.

The exposition is aimed at librarians, archivists, computer scientists, and other professionals interested in modeling bibliographic descriptions as linked data. It aims to achieve a balanced treatment of theory, technical detail, and practical application.

KEYWORDS

Library, Semantic Web, Library metadata, Resource description, Ontology development, Schema.org

Contents

Preface

OCLC is a nonprofit library cooperative providing research, programs, and services that help libraries share the world's knowledge. OCLC manages WorldCat, the largest and most comprehensive catalog of library resources from around the world. In the time period covered by this book, WorldCat contained more than 300 million bibliographic records that represented more than 2 billion items held by participating libraries. OCLC is also the custodian of the Dewey Decimal Classification, which has been used by libraries for over a hundred years to organize their collections. In addition, OCLC hosts the Virtual International Authority File, or VIAF, the largest aggregation of authoritative information collected by libraries about people and organizations and the creative works they have published. Resources such as these make it easier for libraries to fulfill their public mission of connecting library patrons to the works that satisfy their quest for information.

OCLC Research was founded in 1978 and has made significant contributions to the development of the library and Web standards that form the conceptual underpinning of WorldCat and other library resources. In the mid-1990s, OCLC researchers began making the case that libraries need to be integrated into the Web, because that's where the information seekers are. As Semantic Web technologies have matured, this argument has only become more urgent.

OCLC researchers have participated in the Library Linked Data Incubator Group sponsored by the World Wide Web Consortium. They have been vocal members of the Schema Bib Extend Community Group, which recommends extensions to Schema.org, the indexing vocabulary recommended by Google, Yahoo, Bing, and Yandex. OCLC researchers have also worked with the Wikipedia community to facilitate the cross-directional linking between library resources and Wikipedia articles. The results guide human readers from Wikipedia to libraries and enable machine processes to consume richer linked data through Wikipedia's association with the Wikidata project. In addition, OCLC researchers have served as advisers to the BIBFRAME standard sponsored by the Library of Congress, whose goal is to replace MARC, the legacy standard for bibliographic description, with a linked data model. And in the past five years, OCLC has become a significant publisher of linked data, producing models and publicly accessible datasets containing billions of RDF triples describing the objects and concepts referenced in VIAF; the Dewey Decimal Classification, or DDC; Faceted Application of Subject Headings, or FAST; and the WorldCat catalog. It is from this rich experience that this volume emerges.

This book is about OCLC's experiments in the redesign of traditional library resource descriptions as linked data. In practical terms, the goal of the work reported in this book is to define the first draft of an entity-relationship model of creative works and the events in the library community that impact them. The model is realized by mining the data stores maintained at OCLC and republishing them as large RDF datasets. Though the work is necessarily anchored to a particular point in time, we hope that readers will gain insight into the collective thinking of the world's largest library cooperative, whose solutions will spur development by others who might benefit from our trials and errors as well as our successes. In a program whose goal is to express library metadata as linked data, we are doing work that is consistent with the core values of our profession, which places a premium on collaboration and openness. In return, we are confident that the Web of Data will be enriched by the collective expertise of over a hundred years of librarianship.

The impetus for this book arose from a 2012 conversation between Lorcan Dempsey, OCLC Vice President of Research and Chief Strategist, and Ying Ding, Associate Professor of Information Science at Indiana University. The outcome was an invitation to propose a monograph for the series *Synthesis Lectures on the Semantic Web: Theory and Technology* published by Morgan and Claypool. Once the proposal was accepted, Jean Godby, Senior Research Scientist with OCLC Research, was tasked with organizing contributions from colleagues and contributing to the volume herself. Beginning in 2013 and stretching into the first half of 2014, material was contributed, refined, and in some cases re-written as work in progress at OCLC as researchers and their technical allies moved forward. In describing OCLC's projects, the aim is to tell a story about a large collection of interconnected projects. Each chapter is designed as a lecture on a problem that must be addressed if the enterprise of transforming library data to a format that is more effective at fulfilling the needs of the information-seeking public is to succeed.

Many OCLC colleagues have contributed intellectual content in addition to the three authors of this book: Lorcan Dempsey, Jonathan Fausey, Ted Fons, Janifer Gatenby, Thom Hickey, Maximilian Klein, Michael Panzer, Tod Matola, Ed O'Neill, Stephan Schindehette, Jenny Toves, Diane Vizine-Goetz, Richard Wallis, and Jeff Young. The authors are especially indebted to Karen Smith-Yoshimura, whose own important contributions to research on library metadata and whose thoughtful comments on the entire manuscript produced so many improvements that we realize, in hindsight, that she should have been a co-author. We are also grateful to OCLC colleagues who helped us with editorial and production tasks, including Eric Childress, Chris Galvin, Brad Gauder, Jenny Johnson, Jeanette McNichol, and JD Shipengrover.

In addition, we have benefited from engagement with colleagues in the library community, who mentored us, commented on the manuscript, tested some of our ideas at their own institutions, and joined with us in lengthy and often passionate discussion that produced many photos of whiteboards, some of which have found their way into the illustrations in this book. In particular, we are grateful to Kenning Arlitsch, Montana State University; Ray Denenberg, Library of Congress; Ying Ding, Indiana University; Kevin Ford, formerly of the Library of Congress; Paul Groth, Vrije Universiteit Amsterdam; Antoine Isaac, Vrije Universiteit Amsterdam; Nannette Naught, IMT Associates; Patrick OBrien, Montana State University; Philip Schreur, Stanford University; and Marcia Zeng, Kent State University. And of course, we are deeply indebted to our former OCLC colleagues Eric Miller and Stu Weibel, without whose groundbreaking work this enterprise might never have taken shape.

Carol Jean Godby, Shenghui Wang, and Jeffrey K. Mixter
March 2015

CHAPTER 1

Library Standards and the Semantic Web

1.1 THE WEB OF DOCUMENTS AND THE SEMANTIC WEB

"Most of the Web's content today is designed for humans to read, not for computer programs to manipulate meaningfully. Computers can adeptly parse Web pages for layout and routine processing—here a header, there a link to another page—but in general, computers have no reliable way to process the semantics: this is the home page of the Hartman and Strauss Physio Clinic, this link goes to Dr. Hartman's curriculum vitae.

The Semantic Web will bring structure to the meaningful content of Web pages, creating an environment where software agents roaming from page to page can readily carry out sophisticated tasks for users. …[It] is not a separate Web but an extension of the current one, in which information is given well-defined meaning, better enabling computers and people to work in cooperation. The first steps in weaving the Semantic Web into the structure of the existing Web are already under way. In the near future, these developments will usher in significant new functionality as machines become much better able to process and 'understand' the data that they merely display at present." (Berners-Lee, Hendler, and Lasilla 2001)

Readers in 2001 might have read this account of the Semantic Web as science fiction, especially the details of how it would be put to use. In the same passage, the authors describe a hypothetical scenario featuring a ringing phone that lowers the volume of nearby devices so its human owner can take an urgent call from a physician, followed up with the complex logistics of arranging appointments and prescriptions for an aging parent. These details are managed automatically by robots roaming across a smarter Web to collect names, addresses, and ratings of nearby health-care providers and insurance companies.

Fourteen years later, this scenario might be interpreted as an edge-case application of the Semantic Web, but is not especially far-fetched. It depends on the transformation of the Web from a collection of documents that are displayed to a human reader to a network of structured data that is associated with real things in the world, such as patients, physicians, pharmacies, and schedules. Thus, in some limited sense, structured data can be understood and acted upon by algorithmic processes that do something useful. Less dramatic applications of the Semantic Web data architecture are now part of everyday experience. They offer invisible assistance to a traveler wishing to locate highly rated farm-to-table restaurants in a strange city, a shopper wanting to buy a gallon of Benjamin Moore's 'Guilford Green' from the closest paint store, and a student searching Google for the basic facts about William Henry Harrison, the ninth President of the United States. A plausible addition to this list is an improved Web experience that would make libraries and their collections more prominent and accessible to the information-seeking public. This book is a progress report on that goal, focusing on OCLC's experiments with metadata managed by libraries using the conventions of linked data, the latest convention for realizing the promise of the Semantic Web.

1.1.1   RECORDS AND GRAPHS

A more concrete discussion can begin with picture of a document that should be familiar to librarians, publishers, and information seekers, and its reformulation as a network of structured data. Figure 1.1 shows a simplified view of the 'before' and 'after' formats for a description of a paperback edition of Shakespeare's *Hamlet* published by Penguin Books in 1994. Above the blue, book-shaped icon near the bottom of the figure is a record representing the work, which lists its author, title, publisher, publication date, ISBN, and page count. Records in this format can be extracted from nearly all published standards for bibliographic description and are ubiquitous in library catalogs, OCLC's WorldCat catalog data, and bookseller websites such as Amazon.com. Extending upward from the record along multicolored paths, the same information is encoded as a labeled graph that distills the essential meaning of the document. Though the output might appear stilted to a human reader, the information captured in the graph can be assembled into atomic statements such as 'Penguin Books is the name of an Organization,' 'Penguin Books is the publisher of *Hamlet*,' 'William Shakespeare is the name of a person,' 'William Shakespeare is the author of *Hamlet*,' 'An edition of *Hamlet* has the publication date 1994,' 'Penguin Books is located in a place,' 'New York is the name of a place,' and so on. Each statement associates nouns—or 'entities'—such as 'William Shakespeare' or 'Hamlet' with a verb or verb phrase of some kind–or 'relationships'—such as 'is the author of,' to create what computer scientists call an 'entity-relationship' graph.

For the past eight years, OCLC researchers have been working with library standards communities to define entity-relationship models for the description of resources managed by libraries and implement them on a large scale in OCLC's publicly accessible databases. Newcomers to this project often ask whether the result is a new view or an enhancement of existing formats, or a new model altogether; and, more importantly, why the difference in representation matters.

We can formulate a rough draft of an answer to these questions by taking a closer look at Figure 1.1. A human reader can infer from the human-readable description at the bottom of the image that William Shakespeare is a person who wrote something named *Hamlet*, which was published in 1994 by a company named Penguin Books. The reader might have learned in a literature class or an encyclopedia article that William Shakespeare was a man who lived in

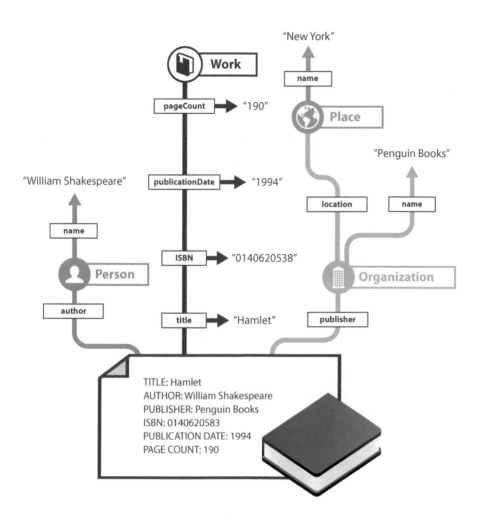

Figure 1.1: A bibliographic description as a record and a graph.

England in the 1500s. The same authoritative sources would also enable a reader to learn that *Hamlet* is a play originally written in verse in a form of English that contemporary readers consider archaic, and is one of Shakespeare's most famous works. Readers who wish to obtain a copy of this edition of *Hamlet* might make an intelligent guess that if it is a typical product from Penguin Books, it is a small, inexpensive paperback volume that can be obtained from a library or bookseller by entering the ISBN into an order form, typically through a Web interface. Thus the human reader can assign an actionable interpretation to the description at the bottom of the image. But a machine cannot. The largest obstacle is that such records consist primarily of text that must be parsed and interpreted with the help of real-world knowledge, a task that outstrips the capabilities of the current generation of natural language processing software.

To compensate, data scientists have been designing entity-relationship models since the 1970s. By reducing the complexity of natural language to manageable sets of nouns and verbs that are well-defined and unambiguous, sentence-like statements can be interpreted without the need for computationally expensive and error-prone process operating literally on human-readable text. What emerges from this exercise is a formal model of a restricted domain from which a network of self-contained statements with a machine-understandable semantics can be generated. In the small domain defined by Figure 1.1, for example, William Shakespeare would be mentioned in other statements about authorship because he created many works in addition to *Hamlet*. So would the city of New York, because it is significant for plenty of other reasons important to librarianship besides its location as the corporate headquarters for Penguin Books. The statements that can be generated from the graph shown in Figure 1.1 conform to semantically realistic co-occurrence rules, stipulating that objects are located in a place, or that books have publication dates but organizations do not.

Linked data can be understood as an entity-relationship model with additional requirements. The seminal statement of linked data principles (Berners-Lee 2006), which we discuss in more technical detail in the next section of this chapter, defines linked data as a network of structured statements, or a 'dataset,' expressed using a published vocabulary and a model that identifies entities as things that ordinary people talk about. Put simply, linked data is about things that link to other things. Linked data principles also stipulate the need for authoritative resources about entities—which, for example, associates the sixteenth-century English playwright named 'William Shakespeare' to a persistent Web-accessible link that resolves to machine-understandable identifying information. Encyclopedias and other trusted references satisfy this need in the web of documents, but only humans can read them. The Semantic Web representation can be interpreted as a computational model of those things that humans remember and know to be true. In other words, Semantic Web conventions for describing entities have the effect of promoting a string in a text to a 'thing' in the world. In this formulation, the 'William Shakespeare' mentioned in the description of *Hamlet* shown in Figure 1.1 is correctly identified as the name of the English literary icon and not a dog or a rock band, and represents knowledge about the author of *Hamlet* that endures beyond a single mention in an individual document.

But as Tim Berners-Lee and his coauthors said in the passage quoted at the beginning of this chapter, the Semantic Web is not separate from the web of documents, but an extension of it. Evidence of their coexistence is shown in Figure 1.2, which is a screen capture of a search on Google for *Hamlet* issued in early 2014.

On the left is a ranked list of documents, produced by matching text strings in the user's query using updated versions of decades-old information-retrieval algorithms that encode no understanding of the real world behind the text. On the right is a display built from the Knowledge

Graph, announced by Google in 2012. Sometimes called the 'Knowledge Card,' the display is fundamentally different from the document list because it is about 'Hamlet' the real-world entity, not the text string. It is built by mining facts from data sources such as Freebase (Google 2015), Wikipedia, and the CIA World Factbook (CIA 2015), and reducing them to a composite description featuring only the most reliable information that can be algorithmically discovered. As of 2012, Google had generated Knowledge Cards for 500 million entities, which are populated with 3.5 billion statements extracted from the Knowledge Graph (Google 2012). An experimental upgrade to the Knowledge Graph assembles a network of entities and relationships from a larger variety of inputs and uses machine-learning algorithms to make quality assessments, remove duplicates, merge statements about a given entity from different sources, and draw inferences that can be translated into more machine-processable statements (Dong et al. 2014). Thus the data stores that make up the Semantic Web continue to grow in size and accuracy.

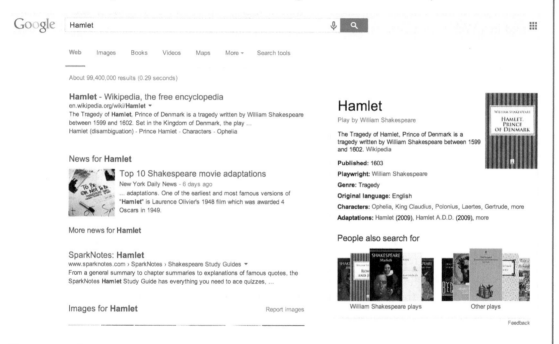

Figure 1.2: Structured and unstructured Google search results for *Hamlet*.

Semantic Web outputs such as the Knowledge Graph are important for three reasons. First, the structured display of the Knowledge Card is easy for users to comprehend and navigate. For example, in the process of building Figure 1.1, algorithms have already determined that the entity in question is Shakespeare's play. Likewise, the Knowledge Card displayed in response to a student's request for information about William Henry Harrison, mentioned earlier, is about the ninth president of the United States. In both cases, information seekers can learn more simply by clicking on the links in the card because the real-world reference has already been resolved. The document list, however, requires the user to evaluate the relevance, veracity, trustworthiness of each item.

Second, a real-world entity, unlike a list of documents, is an object that may be described in multiple data sources or knowledge stores. If the entity is uniquely and publicly identified, these data sources can be merged more easily. This is the key to the smooth operation of the applications of the Semantic Web mentioned in the opening paragraphs of this book: restaurants merged with reviews; a particular kind of paint merged with information about that stores that carry it; and even the complex interactions among physicians, patients, drugs and providers managed by robots that could have been read as science fiction a decade and a half ago.

Finally, entities are natural collection points on the Web for inbound and outbound links involving other entities. Globally important entities such as William Shakespeare the playwright will attract many links because he is mentioned in many resources. In return, globally important entities, and the entities most closely related to them, will be more prominent and thus easier to find in a Web search. This is the same logic that produces ordered lists in the web of documents because those that accumulate the most links are ranked near the top. Thus if William Shakespeare is defined as an entity in the Semantic Web, the creative works by and about him should be more prominent in Web searches, as should the libraries, archives, museums, and booksellers that make these resources available to information seekers. In the domain that is the subject of this book, this is the most useful task that the Semantic Web can accomplish.

Achieving these results in a web of documents has proven intractable, however, because natural language is ambiguous and infinitely variable. As a consequence, the things that people want to know about are too often buried in a sea of text.

1.1.2   THE LINKED DATA CLOUD

In the past five years, the collection of structured datasets conforming to linked data conventions has grown and now represents contributions by many communities of practice, including science, medicine, scholarship, multimedia, government, publishing, and librarianship. In visual terms, the iconic image of the 'Linked Open Data Cloud' maintained by Cyganiac and Jensch (2014) and partially reproduced in Figure 1.3 has become more dense and interconnected. At the center is DBpedia (2015), the structured dataset extracted from Wikipedia, but many other secondary hubs are also visible. For example, GeoNames GN (2014) contains names, images, and geospatial coordinates for 8 million geographic features and 2.5 million populated places; MusicBrainz (MB 2015) is a community-maintained encyclopedia of music; and CiteSeer (PSU 2014) is a digital library of scientific literature. Linked data resources originating from librarians and publishers are shown as green circles in Figure 1.3, which make up about 15% of the total. Among them are some of the most frequently cited datasets in the linked data cloud and represent several projects discussed in this book, including the Library of Congress Subject Headings, the Virtual International Authority File, and WorldCat, as well as projects sponsored by several European libraries.

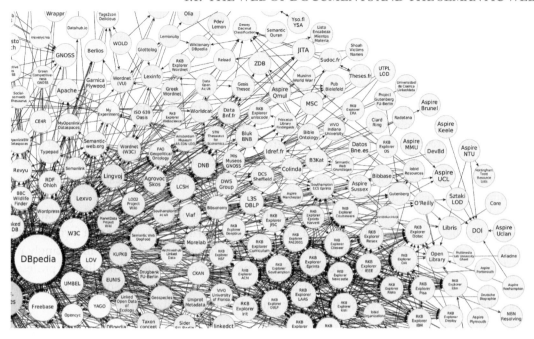

Figure 1.3: Contributions by the library community in the linked data cloud (Cyganiac and Jensch 2014).

In effect, the evolution from the web of documents to the Web of Data defines a new landscape and redefines what it means to publish on the Web. 'What the Web wants,' according to Wallis (2013), is not another database of documents, but large datasets that describe things in the world with authority. They are designed with a familiar structure, a web of links, and entity identifiers that can be mined by third-party data consumers who provide complementary value.

It is common knowledge that most searches for information start not in the library nor even in a Web-accessible library catalog, but elsewhere on the Internet. OCLC's *Perceptions of Libraries* reports document this change in behavior. In 2003, just five years after the appearance of Google, seventy-five percent of college students reported using the Internet more than the library; in 2010, Internet usage had increased among all age groups and was accessible through several kinds of mobile devices (de Rosa et al. 2010). Unfortunately, the contents of library collections are not visible enough on the Web. Fons (2013) argues that libraries perform four functions— acquiring, describing, preserving, and making resources available to patrons—and that current library standards do the first three reasonably well. But reaching users means doing a better job of moving more and richer datasets into the linked data cloud—i.e., exposing library collections on the Web by defining and publishing structured data that describes the important entities and relationships involved in the description of the world's most influential creative works.

The practical goal of the work reported in this book is to define the first draft of an entity-relationship model of creative works and transactions in the library community that impact them, expressing the model in the linked data paradigm. The first outcome is a machine-processable set of statements corresponding to those mentioned at the beginning of this chapter: a Person authors a Work; a Work is 'about' a Concept; a Work is transformed into an Object by a Publisher; a Publisher is an Organization; a Work, Person, Object, or Organization is located in a Place. The model is realized by mining the data stores maintained at OCLC, focusing on the bibliographic descriptions represented in WorldCat, the aggregated catalog of the world's libraries that connects users to hundreds of million books, journals, e-resources, and multimedia objects. The results are published in Schema.org, the vocabulary used by the world's largest search engines to index documents and create structured representations.

In this way, we can satisfy the requirements for the Web of Data by mining large datasets for knowledge about important things in the world and transforming the output to a format that can be understood beyond the library community, where information seekers are increasingly more likely to find it. By doing so, we are exercising some of the core values of the library profession, which places a premium on collaboration and openness. In return, the Web of Data benefits from the collective expertise and authority of over a hundred years of librarianship.

1.2   OCLC'S EXPERIMENTS IN CONTEXT

This section places the concepts we have just described in a larger historical context and sets the stage for a more formal discussion of OCLC's experiments with new models of resource description. Though we will have to retrace a few steps, our goal is to drive the exposition forward with interconnected story lines about the evolution of Web and library standards. But this survey is necessarily selective. For more detail about the Web protocols described here, see (Heath and Bizer 2011). Recent histories of library standards for resource description are recounted in Ford (2012); Fons, Penka, and Wallis (2012), and Kroeger (2013).

Highlights that are discussed in this book are depicted in the timeline shown in Figure 1.4. The right side shows key milestones in the development of Web standards, protocols, and applications, while the left side shows some of the most important reactions by the library standards community. The orange blocks represent the involvement of OCLC, either as managers of high-profile projects, or as leaders in community-driven initiatives. As Figure 1.4 shows, our thumbnail history is divided into three stages: precursors, protocol and standards development, and applications.

1.2.1   WEB STANDARDS FOR DELIVERING DOCUMENTS AND THINGS

In 1991, Tim Berners-Lee announced the birth of the World Wide Web with a document that defined his invention as "a wide-area hypermedia information retrieval initiative aiming to give universal access to a large universe of documents" (WWW 1991). Hypermedia, which includes images and sound, was defined as an extension of hypertext, a term famously coined by Ted

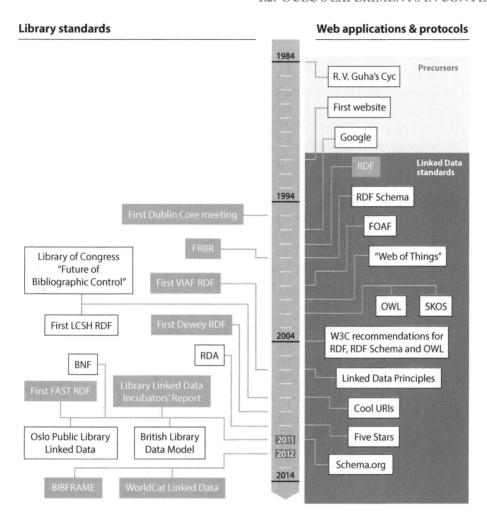

Figure 1.4: Milestones in the development of library linked data.

Nelson 17 years earlier in a self-published book (Nelson 1974). In 1994, Berners-Lee founded the World Wide Web Consortium, or the W3C, an international body for developing standards and engaging in outreach and education. An early priority was the definition of standards and protocols for the structure and semantics of hyperlinks. The URL, or Uniform Resource Locator, is the character string displayed in the address bar of a browser when a document is accessed. The 'URL' concept was quickly absorbed into popular culture, but the broader taxonomy defined two other kinds of links. The URN, or Uniform Resource Name, identified the name of a Web resource independently of its location. The URI, or Uniform Resource Identifier, was the parent term for URLs and URNs that would become the term of choice for referring to the links in linked data (URI-PIG 2001).

Despite the intuitive appeal of the hypermedia browsing experience, Web standards experts realized that knowledge discovery in such an environment is problematic and could be improved by the widespread availability of semantically rich structured data. Thus the Semantic Web was born, and proposals for describing Web-friendly structured data were soon published, many of which matured into formal standards. The Resource Description Framework, or RDF, would become the language of choice for linked data and was already the topic of discussion by multiple and overlapping standards committees in the late 1990s. This discussion produced three important results. First to appear was the 'Resource Description and Framework Model and Syntax' specification (Brickley and Guha 2014), introduced in a progress report in 1997 (Miller and Schloss 1997). The initial draft of the corresponding RDF Schema (Brickley and Guha 2014) was published in 1998 (Brickley, Guha, and Layman 1998). Finally, the Web Ontology Language, or OWL (W3C-OWL 2012), was defined as an expanded formal semantics for RDF and was published as a W3C working draft in 2002 (Dean et al. 2002). All three standards first advanced to W3C recommendation status in 2004 (Klyne and Carroll 2004; Brickley and Guha 2004; Dean and Schreiber 2004).

Metalanguages for describing ontologies in RDF were published only slightly later, two of which are especially important for the models discussed in this book. The Simple Knowledge Organization Scheme, or SKOS (Miles and Bechhofer 2009b), is a lightweight vocabulary for expressing thesauri and other structured vocabularies as RDF, which achieved W3C recommendation status in 2009. The 'Friend of a Friend,' or FOAF ontology (Brickley and Miller 2014), was designed for describing social networks and was first introduced in 2000, several years before linked data principles were published. Though FOAF is not a W3C standard, its importance was recognized by Tim Berners-Lee in 2007, who claimed that "I express my network in a FOAF file, and that is a start of the revolution" (Berners-Lee 2007).

In the next phase, Web standards experts recognized the need to refer not only to a web of hyperlinked documents, but also to a web of 'things' (Berners-Lee 2001). In 2006, Tim Berners-Lee issued the design principles for linked data, stating that "The Semantic Web isn't just about putting data on the web. It is about making links, so that a person or machine can explore the web of data. With linked data, when you have some of it, you can find other, related, data" (Berners-Lee 2006). To realize this vision, Berners-Lee proposed that URIs should refer to things in the world; and that when the URIs are resolved, useful information about these things, including other URIs, should be supplied. As he admits, this is a recommendation for applying the design of Web-accessible thesauri to resources about the people, organizations, places, and concepts that populate the larger universe of Web documents. For example, the user who searches for astronomy in the online version of Wordnet (PU 2013) retrieves a dedicated page with the unique identifier `http://wordnet-online.freedicts.com/definition?word=astronomy`, a definition, and a set of links to broader and narrower terms, such as 'physics,' 'physical science,' 'astrometry,' and 'solar physics.' According to Berners-Lee, a linked data resource about William Shakespeare should offer the same kind of information. To accomplish this goal, " Sauermann and Cyganiac (2007) argue in the document "Cool URIs for the Semantic Web" Sauermann and Cyganiac (2007) that a 'real-world object—or, more commonly, a 'thing'—is different from a Web-accessible document about it, and define Web protocols to encode the distinction.

Figure 1.5: Five-star data (from Berners-Lee 2006, updated in 2010).

In 2010, Berners-Lee published an update to his 2006 document with what would become a widely reproduced and iconic image: the coffee cup with five stars, shown in Figure 1.5. The cup, and the accompanying explanation, can be interpreted as a graduated list of technical and accessibility requirements for realizing the full linked data vision. From a technical perspective, the goal is a set of globally unique URIs to real-world things, related to one another through relationships expressed in a domain model, which is coded in RDF using published vocabularies that can be consumed by third parties. Independent of these requirements is the declaration of a professional ethic promoting the value of machine-readable data in a non-proprietary format that is openly accessible on the Web. Together, the five stars imply that data stores of the highest quality are fully open as well as linked, and represent a checklist that is routinely applied to linked data projects, including OCLC's.

By 2011, the design principles of linked data were established well enough that Google, Yahoo, Bing, and Yandex could announce the publication of Schema.org, the comprehensive vocabulary that these search engines would use for indexing Web pages and creating structured data, such as the Google Knowledge Graphs we have already mentioned. Though the appearance of Schema.org was perceived as abrupt at the time, the groundwork had prepared through decades of research in knowledge engineering. The primary author was R.V. Guha, who based it on the comprehensive ontology Cyc, which was first introduced in the 1970s (Lenant and Guha 1989). During the formative years of the Semantic Web, Guha also worked behind the scenes to improve the most important standards, particularly the RDF Schema (Brickley and Guha 2014).

Looking back on his experience in 2014, Guha observed that despite the growing sophistication of the Semantic Web standards, fewer than 1,000 sites were using these standards to produce structured data even as late as 2004. Still missing was a value proposition aimed at webmasters that promises greater visibility and more easily navigable displays to those who make structured data available to search engines. To paraphrase the text on a slide from a recent presentation, Schema.org permits simple things to be simple and complex things to be possible (Guha 2014). Schema.org markup is now being published by major sites in a variety of sectors, including news, e-commerce, sports, medicine, music, real estate, and employment. The vocabulary is managed through direct engagement with communities of practice and moderated discussion on W3C lists.

1.2.2   THE LIBRARY COMMUNITY RESPONDS

Largely in response to the evolution of the Web in the 1990s as a compelling platform for free access to high-quality information, library standards were also undergoing major change. In 1995, members of the library and Internet standards communities assembled in 1995 for the inaugural Dublin Core meeting, less than a year after the first World Wide Web conference. They argued that a lightweight version of librarians' descriptive standards should be applied to Web documents to facilitate discovery (Weibel et al. 1995). This focus on description evolved into an interest in structured data and early leadership roles by members of the library community in the development of RDF. For example, Eric Miller, who worked as a research scientist at OCLC on the initial RDF specifications, later served as the Semantic Web Activity Lead for the World Wide Web Consortium.

In the broader library community, the Web was recognized as a disruptive technology that could either help libraries or threaten them with obsolescence. In a survey of the new landscape, Dempsey et al. (2005) explored the implications for the discovery and description of library resources. Since, as the authors pointed out, "...for many users, Google and other search engines are increasingly becoming the first and last search result," it would be necessary to manage metadata encoded in library-community standards alongside a much greater diversity of structured and semi-structured text. In addition, the key references maintained by the library community—such as vocabularies, authority files, and mappings among metadata standards—would have to be recast in Web-friendly formats to leverage their value in an environment that integrates libraries with the Internet at large. If these challenges cannot be met, the authors argued, the most valuable library resources would be lost in a sea of other options.

A sense of urgency was also conveyed in the report published in 2008 by the Library of Congress, *On the Record*, which permeated all aspects of librarianship, but was especially acute in the domain of data standards and technical infrastructure. By then, it was widely recognized that MARC (or Machine-Readable Cataloging) and the other first-generation standards that had brought libraries into the computer age starting in the 1960s were nearing the end of their useful lives. The authors of the report concluded that "the World Wide Web is both our technology platform and the appropriate platform for the delivery of our standards" and that "people are not the only users of the data we produce in the name of bibliographic control, but so too are machine applications that interact with those data in a variety of ways" (LC 2008b).

After the publication of *On the Record*, the Library of Congress formed the Bibliographic Framework Transition Initiative, a working group that recommended the use of entity-relationship models such Functional Requirements for Bibliographic Description, or FRBR (IFLA-SG 1998), and Resource Description and Access, or RDA (RDA 2010). The same group sponsored the development of BIBFRAME (LC 2014b), a linked-data compatible model of bibliographic description that was positioned as a replacement for MARC and would be published as an early draft in 2012. During the same period, library standards experts developed RDF-encoded abstract models (DCMI 2007), created repositories of Web-accessible ontologies and vocabularies such as the Open Metadata Registry (OMR 2014), and built Web-friendly models for nontraditional resources managed by libraries and other cultural heritage institutions—for example, the Europeana Data Model (Europeana 2014). Much of this activity can be interpreted as anticipatory, but as soon as the Web protocols for linked data were mature enough to support the publication of large data stores, many important library authority files were redesigned for the new architecture, including the Library of the Congress Subject Headings, or LCSH (Summers et al. 2008); the Virtual International Authority File, or VIAF (VIAF 2014); the Faceted Application of Subject Terms, or FAST (OCLC 2011b); and the top-level hierarchies in the Dewey Decimal Classification (Panzer and Zeng 2009).

1.2.3   LINKED DATA IN WORLDCAT

The projects described in this book emerged from 2011 and 2012, two especially productive years. In 2011, the W3C-sponsored Library Linked Data Incubator Group published a consensus statement (Baker et al. 2011). Among the Incubators were many of the leaders of the projects reported in the publications cited above, including OCLC's Jeff Young, the chief architect of OCLC's published linked data, and Michael Panzer, Editor in Chief of the Dewey Decimal Classification.

The Incubators' statement is grounded in two critical observations. First, they argue that "Linked data builds on the defining feature of the Web: browsable links (URIs) spanning a seamless information space." They also recognize that "Linked data is not about creating a different Web, but rather about enhancing the Web through the addition of structured data." The report also lists the arguments for the production and consumption of linked data by libraries, describes the status of the linked data projects in the library community as of 2011, and identifies obstacles to progress. In essence, the Incubators argued that linked data is consistent with the core values of librarianship that emphasize the collaborative creation of metadata and the open sharing of resources. The new architecture simply sets a higher standard for acting on these values. Linked data design principles stipulate that resource descriptions contain globally unique identifiers and be capable of machine interpretation outside their original community of practice. The Incubators' report points out that these requirements were first demonstrated to be feasible in the conversion of library authority files. But bibliographic description is a much larger challenge because of the larger scope of the standards; MARC alone can express thousands of concepts, which are encoded primarily as human-readable text (Smith-Yoshimura et al. 2010). Karen Coyle, an Incubator, prescribes a ladder of success from text to machine-processable data (Coyle 2012) that can be interpreted as a set of steps for upgrading bibliographic metadata to five-star linked data, following Tim Berners-Lee's 2010 recommendations.

While the Incubators' report was being prepared, there were other major developments. First, the British Library published a data model, accompanied by a dataset that described all 2.5 million resources in the British National Bibliography (Hodson et al. 2012), producing the largest and most sophisticated linked data implementation of library bibliographic description to date. Second, the entire catalog of the Oslo Public Library was published as linked data (Rekkavik 2014). Finally, Schema.org was published. By then, OCLC's research team was engaged in the task of creating linked data for the entire collection of WorldCat catalog data. Since our initial evaluation of Schema.org consisted of relabeling some of the descriptions available from the British Library dataset, which we describe in more detail in Chapter 3, we concluded that Schema.org is rich enough to accomplish the same goals and has the considerable added benefit of being consumable by the world's major search engines.

In 2012, an experimental draft of a linked data model for bibliographic description derived from Schema.org was published as RDFa markup, an RDF syntax that is compatible with HTML (Herman, Adida, and Sporny 2013), on approximately 300,000,000 HTML-encoded MARC records accessible from WorldCat.org. These descriptions contained URIs linking to RDF datasets that represent the Dewey Decimal Classification, the Library of Congress Subject Headings, the Library of Congress Name Authority File, VIAF, and FAST. By orders of magnitude, this was the largest set of linked library bibliographic data expressed "…in the form the Web wants," in terms of scale, a familiar structure, a network of links, and entity identifiers. The significance of this achievement was highlighted in a press release (OCLC 2012): "Adding linked data to WorldCat records makes those records more useful—especially to search engines, developers, and services on the wider Web, beyond the library community. This will make it easier for search engines to connect non-library organizations to library data." In 2014, these descriptions were significantly enhanced by the addition of URIs from WorldCat Works (OCLC 2014d), an RDF dataset that is automatically generated from WorldCat catalog records and identifies common content in the editions and formats of particular books, sound recordings, and other resources held in library collections.

The next section of this chapter walks through a sample description, starting from a user's search on WorldCat.org. The rest of the book is about the development of authoritative resource hubs for the key entities that stand behind such descriptions, making it possible to envision a maturation of the initial experiments into a next-generation platform for library resource description. As our projects mature, our commitment in Schema.org has only solidified. Though Schema.org offers the promise of greater visibility by search engines, it is also a large, extensible, and growing vocabulary that is compatible with the goals of linked data and can be interpreted as a de-facto standard. According to an informal estimate offered by R.V. Guha (Dataversity 2013) in late 2013, Schema.org markup has been published on approximately 15% of the Web pages processed by Google. When we started to model bibliographic resources in 2011, there were no other realistic options, either in library standards or in vocabularies published outside the library community that had a comparable scope, depth, institutional support, and adoption rate.

As we have already noted, the first draft of the BIBFRAME model was also published by the Library of Congress in 2012. This is an important milestone in the development of linked data for bibliographic description because it represents a commitment to linked data by one of the most important institutions in the international library community. According to Kevin Ford, a key BIBFRAME architect, "Linked data is about sharing data ..." and "...provides a strong and well-defined means to communicate library data, one of the main functions requiring attention in the community's migration from MARC" (Ford 2012), a point that McCallum (2015) elaborates.

OCLC was invited to participate in the BIBFRAME Early Experimenters' Group, which was active in 2012 and 2013. Both in closed and public meetings, we have argued that OCLC's models are compatible but complementary (Godby 2013). The two models have similar primary concepts such as 'Work,' 'Person,' and 'Organization.' But BIBFRAME is being developed as the replacement for MARC, addressing the need for data exchange among libraries in the Semantic Web.

OCLC's modeling experiments address the problem of integrating library resources in the broader Web. During the past year, while this manuscript was being prepared, the projects led by the Library of Congress and OCLC have advanced in parallel. The Library of Congress has developed the BIBFRAME Implementation Testbed (LC 2015), which includes conversion tools and a discussion forum for interacting with 17 organizations who are conducting pilot tests. OCLC has not participated in the BIBFRAME pilot tests, but has focused instead on refining the models and implementation details described in the following chapters. Though our conclusion about the two modeling initiaves has not changed since 2013, OCLC has begun to collaborate with the Library of Congress to gain a deeper understanding of how the models interoperate. This effort was taking shape too late to be discussed in this book, but Godby and Denenberg (2015) provides a high-level summary of a technical analysis that will be published later in 2015.

1.3 A TECHNICAL INTRODUCTION

A bibliographic record accessible from WorldCat.org describes a creative work for a library patron who wishes to discover and perhaps gain access to it. Figure 1.6 shows a record for the book *American Guerrilla: My War Behind Japanese Lines*, which was written by Roger Hilsman and published in 2005 by Potomac Books in Washington, DC, as member of the series *Memories of War*, which includes other memoirs about World War II that can be discovered by clicking on the link beside the 'Series:' label.

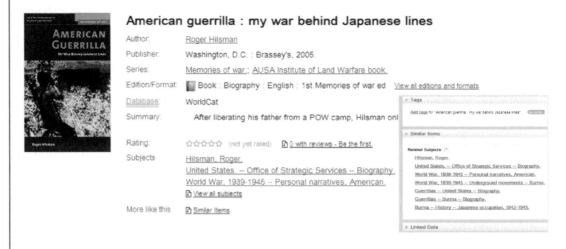

Figure 1.6: An excerpt from a WorldCat.org display for a World War II memoir. WorldCat ID 52347585.

This is only the first segment of the description of *American Guerrilla* accessible from WorldCat.org, the search interface for the WorldCat catalog. Additional segments provide links to reviews, to the websites of nearby libraries that own the book, to online booksellers such as Barnes & Noble and Amazon.com, and to details that might help the reader obtain the book, such as a physical description and the ISBN 1574886916. Patrons who click on the 'Similar Items' link shown on the right side of Figure 1.6 can view this description in the larger web of creative works to which librarians have assigned the same subject headings. It is thus possible to discover a video interview of Roger Hilsman produced by a public broadcasting station based in Boston in 1981, a Ph.D. dissertation submitted to the University of Arkansas in 1999, and many other works about guerrillas in Burma, the Japanese occupation of Burma from 1939–1945, and World War II itself.

The labels on this page from the WorldCat.org interface are available in English and ten other languages. It is a patron-friendly view of a MARC record and is enhanced with RDF statements that can be viewed in a human-readable format from the 'Linked Data' section at the bottom of the page, as shown in the inset on the right side of the figure. There is nothing particularly unusual about this description, except that the source record is easy enough for casual readers to understand but complex enough to be interesting and permits us to draw some comparisons with the British Library Data Model in a later chapter. In addition, *American Guerrilla* is a relatively obscure book that can be contrasted with more famous creative works whose more complex publication histories illustrate issues that the OCLC model is being designed to address, and we will mention it a few more times in subsequent chapters. But in the rest of this section, our goal is to work through the WorldCat description excerpted in Figure 1.7 in deeper levels of detail, ending with a high-level understanding of the RDF markup and a sense of the work that remains to be done.

1.3.1   FROM A MARC 21 RECORD TO RDF

Figure 1.7 is an excerpt of the corresponding MARC 21 record, which conforms to the standard defined in the MARC 21 Format for Bibliographic Data maintained by the Library of Congress (LC 2014e). The 100 $a field states that Roger Hilsman is the author, while the 245, 250, 260, and 300 fields contain details about the title, edition, imprint, and physical format of the published book. The 490 $a field lists the title of the publisher-defined series to which this book belongs, *Memories of War*. Other titles in the series include *War in the Boats: My World War II Submarine Battles* and *Wake Island Pilot: A World War II Memoir*, which are also described in WorldCat. The 500 and 520 fields contain free-text or lightly formatted notes. The subject headings listed in the 600, 610, and 650 fields are derived from Library of Congress subject headings, except for *Guerrilla*, whose source is not specified in this excerpt. Finally, the 082 field contains a number defined from components of Edition 21 of the Dewey Decimal Classification, which was constructed to capture the subject of this book with enough precision to place it on a library shelf among books with similar topics.

The first task required for converting the MARC record to RDF exploits the obvious correspondences between the semantics of the MARC 21 fields and subfields with the terms defined in Schema.org. Table 1.1 shows a small sample that is relevant to the record shown in Figure 1.7. At this point in the discussion, even before we examine the RDF statements, it is possible to make several broad observations. First, lexical mappings to and from MARC are constantly being defined for the important international Web-friendly standards that have appeared since the 1990s ((LC 2008a, 2014f; EDItEUR 2009)), whose meaning is also theoretically expressible using set-theoretic relationships defined in OWL (Dunsire et al. 2011) instead of source-target tables, or metadata crosswalks, such as the one shown below. Second, this exercise has convinced many library standards experts (Ronallo 2012), including those at OCLC, that Schema.org is a reasonable starting point for the description of library resources on the Web.

Finally, this exercise already points to the need for an analysis that goes beyond lexical substitution because the conversion from MARC to RDF requires more than simple relabeling. Following established practice in the linked data community, we represent names of classes – or entities – defined in a Semantic Web vocabulary with a capitalized first letter, such as schema:CreativeWork, while properties – or relationships – are represented with a lower-case first letter. All of the terms shown in Table 1.1 are properties defined in schema:CreativeWork, though the use of schema:isPartOf is unsatisfactory for reasons we discuss below. The semantics of the MARC record permit a reader to infer that a schema:creator or schema:contributor is a relationship between a person or organization and a creative work. But the literal references to these

082 00	$a 940.54.8673/092 $a B $2 21l
100 1_	$a Hilsman, Roger.
245	$a American guerrilla : $b my war behind Japanese lines $c Roger Hilsman
250	$a 1st Memories of war ed.
260	$a Washington, D.C. : $b Brasseys, $c 2005
300	$a 312 p.
490	$a Memories of war
500	$a Includes index.
520	$a After liberating his father from a POW camp, Hilsman only heard, "What took you so long?"
600 10	$a Hilsman, Roger
610 10	$a United States. $b Office of Strategic Services $v Biography
650 _0	$a World War, 1939-1945 $v Personal narratives, American
650 _7	$a Guerrilla
650 _0	$a Guerrillas $z United States $v Biography
650 _0	$a Guerrillas $z Burma $v Biography
651 _0	$a Burma $x History $y Japanese occupation, 1942-1945
653	$a Office of Strategic Services

Figure 1.7: Excerpts from a MARC record describing *American Guerrilla*.

Table 1.1: Lexical substitutions from MARC 21 to Schema.org

MARC 21 Source	Schema.org Target
100, 110 $a	schema:creator
700 $a	schema:contributor
245 $a	schema:name
260 $c	schema:datePublished
260 $b	schema:publisher
300 $a	schema:numberOfPages
490 $a	schema:isPartOf
500 $a	schema:description
600, 610, 630, 650 $a	schema:about

classes, which are required links to the real-world entities in a bibliographic description, are only assumed. The same point can be made about simpler properties such as schema:description or schema:numberOfPages, which are two-way relationships between a creative work and a literal string. A formal model is required to acknowledge these classes and properties explicitly, a topic we discuss in detail in Chapter 3.

```
@prefix schema: <http://schema.org/>.
@prefix rdf: <http://www.w3.org/1999/02/22-rdf-syntax-ns#>.
@prefix owl: <http://www.w3.org/2002/07/owl#>.
@prefix madsrdf: <http://www.loc.gov/standards/mads/rdf/>.
@prefix library: <http://purl.org/library/>.


<http://www.worldcat.org/oclc/52347585>
a schema:Book ;
    owl:sameAs <info:oclcnum/52347585> ;
    schema:name "American guerrilla : my war behind Japanese lines" ;
    schema:author <http://viaf.org/viaf/37001878> ;
    schema:publisher [a schema:Organization; schema:name "Brassey's"] ;
    schema:bookEdition "1st Memories of war ed." ;
    schema:inLanguage "en" ;
    schema:numberOfPages "312" ;
    schema:datePublished "2005" ;
    schema:isPartOf "Memories of war" ;
    schema:about <http://viaf.org/viaf/37001878> ;
    schema:about <http://id.loc.gov/authorities/subjects/sh85057696> ;
    schema:about <http://viaf.org/viaf/150910486> ;
    schema:about [a schema:Intangible "Office of Strategic Services"] ;
    schema:about <http://id.worldcat.org/fast/948935>.

<http://id.loc.gov/authorities/subjects/sh85057696>
a schema:Intangible ;
    schema:name "Guerrillas–Burma" .

<http://viaf.org/viaf/37001878>
a schema:Person ;
    schema:name "Hilsman, Roger" ;
    madsrdf:IsIdentifiedByAuthority <http://id.loc.gov/authorities/names/n50034436> .

<http://viaf.org/viaf/150910486>
a schema:Organization;
    schema:name "United States. Office of Strategic Services" ;
    madsrdf:isIdentifiedByAuthority <http://id.loc.gov/authorities/names/n80030466> .
```

Figure 1.8: An RDF/Turtle description of *American Guerrilla*.

The RDF markup corresponding to Figure 1.6 is shown in Figure 1.8. It is expressed in the Turtle syntax (Beckett and Berners-Lee 2011), which we use throughout the book because it is only slightly more difficult to read than a Dublin Core description and can be converted mechanically to richer RDF formats using a Web-accessible translator such as RDFLib (Stolz 2014). In Figure 1.8, the main segments in the description are separated by whitespace. From top to bottom, they are the namespace declaration, the primary description, and four secondary descriptions. The namespace declaration contains references to RDF and OWL, the expected RDF infrastructure, and to Schema.org. The namespace 'madsRDF' refers to the model of library authority files maintained by the Library of Congress (LC 2012), which is slightly richer than SKOS, a topic we discuss briefly in Chapter 2.

The primary and secondary 'description' blocks represent <rdf:Description> statements and have the same structure. The first line is a URI reference to a real-world object; the second line starts with 'a' and represents the <rdf:type> declaration for the object; and the last line is a period marking the end of the block. The intervening statements identify properties of the object being described. In Figure 1.8, the URI <http://www.worldcat.org/oclc/52347585> refers to the book *American Guerrilla* authored by Roger Hilsman. The referent of such URIs is ontologically complex, but here it is accurate enough to say that it refers to a schema:Book, which is a subclass of schema:CreativeWork. This book is a concrete object and is associated with a WorldCat Work description of the content, a subtlety that will be described in the model of creative works in Chapter 3. The remaining rdf:Description blocks are conceptually simpler and refer to the people, places, organizations, and topics that have been described in traditional library authority files, many of which have been modeled as linked data. This is the subject of Chapter 2.

The rdf:Description blocks exhibit different degrees of technical maturity, which can be read off the format of the data in the predicate. Those with URIs are the most fully realized. For example, the same VIAF identifier is a predicate of schema:author and schema:about, which resolves to the person named Roger Hilsman who wrote *American Guerrilla*, a restatement of the fact that a memoir is both by and about the author. In the corresponding subordinate description, the property madsrdf:isIdentifiedbyAuthority is used to state that the same person has also been described in the Library of Congress Name Authorities file. In sum, these statements identify Roger Hilsman as a unique individual, establish his identity through a persistent URI, and aggregate information about him from multiple published sources.

RDF predicates containing quoted strings, however, are red flags in the linked data paradigm. They need more attention. Though some, such as titles and descriptions, are intrinsic string literals that require no further processing, most of the others represent strings that have not yet been promoted to 'things.' This is true even if the predicate is a string whose RDF type and properties can be inferred from the MARC source. For example, the compound statement schema:about [a schema:Intangible "Office of Strategic Services"] is mapped to Schema.org as an 'intangible thing' from a MARC 653 field, indicating that the string has no source in a library authority file. Thus the RDF statement is no more informative than the MARC source. Nevertheless, evidence exists elsewhere in the record that 'Office of Strategic Services' is modeled as an organization in the linked data version of FAST, where it is associated with a persistent URI. A human reader can detect this redundancy, but a simple machine process cannot. Likewise, the slightly more complex statement schema:publisher [a schema:Organization; schema:name "Brassey's"] is a paraphrase of the MARC 260 $b description of a publisher as an organization with a particular name. But 'Brasesy's' is still a string and not the name of a recognizable real-world thing because it is not linked by a URI to a description in an authoritative entity hub. A more sophisticated data-mining process would discover that 'Brassey's' is the name of a publisher and is associated with URIs in several library authority files that have been modeled as linked data.

The statement schema:isPartOf "Memories of War" exposes another unfinished task. The statement uses the property isPartOf, defined for schema:Thing, to describe *American Guerrilla* as a member of a series. But *Memories of War* is a collection, not a single creative work, a fact that cannot be expressed in the current version of Schema.org. Problems such as this one are being addressed by the W3C-sponsored Schema Bib Extend Community Group (Schema Bib Extend 2014d), whose membership includes representatives from OCLC and the broader library and publisher metadata standards communities. This group has been convened with the purpose of proposing extensions to Schema.org that would be formally included in the standard. Discussion is underway to define Collection more generically as a subclass of schema:Thing and deprecate the already defined schema:CollectionPage, which applies only to schema:WebPage, a subclass of schema:CreativeWork (Schema Bib Extend 2014a). One outcome of this experience is the first draft of an extension vocabulary named BiblioGraph (BGN 2014a), which is formally compatible with Schema.org and contains definitions of classes and properties required for a model of the domain of library resource description that can be shared on the broader Web. These topics are described in detail in Chapter 3.

The URIs shown in Figure 1.8 conform to the Cool URIs convention (Sauermann and Cyganiac 2007), which are simple, stable, manageable, and resolve unambiguously either to an information object or a real-world object. OCLC's URIs resolve only to real-world objects—i.e., to the people, places, organizations, objects, works, and concepts that are referenced in bibliographic descriptions, and not to database records or other documents. Information objects are resolved by the HTTP protocol that returns the status code 200, which we refer to in this book as 'HTTP 200.' A real-world object is identified through the HTTP protocol that redirects the request to a document about the object and returns the 303 status code, which we abbreviate as the 'HTTP 303 redirect.' By implementing the HTTP 303 redirect protocol, the data architect acknowledges that Roger Hilsman himself cannot be delivered when his VIAF identifier is dereferenced, but an authoritative document about him can be delivered instead—namely, a VIAF description, which we discuss in Chapter 2. The Cool URIs convention also makes it possible to define seemingly unreal things such as concepts, ghosts, and unicorns as real-world objects if the Web can be viewed as a corpus of documents and there is some consensus about what they refer to. Thus, a document request resolved with an HTTP 303 redirect can be used to define a kind of machine-processable reference by denotation, as Panzer (2012) argues.

1.3.2   MANAGING ENTITIES IN THE WEB OF DATA

Stepping back from the minute details of the above example, we can observe that nearly all of a reasonably complex MARC 21 bibliographic record can be rendered as some form of linked data, labeled primarily with vocabulary defined in Schema.org. URIs replace most of the strings in the source record and are resolved by a protocol that recognizes the real-world objects in the description. This is a success story and a milestone toward the long-term goal of releasing the rich contents of library metadata to a wider population of data consumers both inside and outside the library community.

The linked data paradigm is attractive because successful results offer the promise of machine-understandable data that can be shared on the Web beyond the library community. For the first time in the history of Web data architecture, the linked data paradigm also embodies a computationally realistic theory of reference, encoded in the distinction between the web of documents and the Web of Data.

But the Semantic Web theory of reference is immature and not yet implemented at an actionable scale. Progress requires the identification of real-world objects and the creation of authoritative descriptions, or entity hubs, that are associated with URIs resolved as references to things, not documents. Achieving this goal requires a set of processes that is deeper than the mapping of individual records to Schema.org or other Semantic Web standards because the core problem is to associate a text string such as 'Shakespeare' as the author of *Hamlet* with the playwright who lived in the 16th century in Stratford-upon-Avon, not a rock band, a dog, or the name of a file server. Establishing this connection typically requires the application of data mining algorithms on a corpus of documents. Over time, authoritative entity hubs are enriched as more data publishers contribute their expertise to the identification of globally important entities such as William Shakespeare, 'dark matter,' Google, and Charles Darwin's *The Origin of Species*.

Wikidata and DBpedia can be viewed as early drafts of entity hubs that are already widely referenced. But entity hubs produced from resources managed in the library community are still experimental, though early tests demonstrate that effective prototypes can be derived from authority files and large aggregations of legacy bibliographic descriptions such as WorldCat, the European Library (TEL 2014b), and Europeana (Europeana 2014). But such projects need to be expanded in scope and depth to ensure that resources managed by libraries are more visible to the information-seeking public because they are interconnected with authoritative entity hubs that are highly referenced throughout the Web. This outcome also motivates the design of the LibHub project (Miller 2014), whose goals are congruent with the linked data projects described in this book.

To set a direction that is realistic but ambitious enough to have impact, OCLC has focused the current phase of our work on six key entities—and the web of relationships among them—that can be identified in traditional library authority files and bibliographic records and reformulated as linked data: 'Person,' 'Place,' 'Concept,' Organization,' 'Object,' and 'Work.' More narrowly specified, our goal is to build a baseline proof-of-concept demonstration that establishes common ground with other initiatives in the library standards community by focusing on library resources such as monographs instead of less-well-understood digital and multimedia formats, and focusing more on the publishing of linked data than the consumption of it.

It may be less obvious that our interest in key entities also defines a set of priorities. First, it is a directive to start with where users are—somewhere on the Internet, with an information request. We must build descriptions that do a better job of fulfilling their needs by connecting the expertise now sequestered inside library catalogs to the broader Web using a broadly deployed ontologies such as Schema.org, FOAF, and SKOS, and the W3C-defined protocols for interpreting them. Second, the key entities must be identified, defined in hubs of authoritative information grounded in library descriptive practice, and associated with persistent, globally unique identifiers. This format ensures that the entities are visible to search engines and data providers outside the library community. With respect to current metadata management workflows, these activities can be interpreted as a focus on the representation and architecture of authorities, deferring to the future the more difficult task of reimagining the act of cataloging. Finally, these entities must be interconnected through relationships, or RDF properties, to form a model of the relevant domain.

The projects described in this book have been scoped with an awareness of the progress made so far in library linked data projects. After all, five of the six key entities—all but 'Object'—make up the content of traditional library authority files, for which linked data models were first defined and are now commonplace. OCLC's contributions to this effort are the subject of Chapter 2 and culminate with a description of VIAF, whose semantics have evolved beyond that of the traditional library authority file to an authoritative hub with inbound and outbound links to the broader Web. Chapter 3 reports on a set of projects that recognize the user's understanding of a Work such as *Hamlet* as an abstract information request and interprets its various physical realizations as Objects that offer a range of fulfillment options. The result is a lightweight and flexible model of creative works inspired by the conceptual model for the Functional Requirements for Bibliographic Records, or FRBR, and expressed primarily in Schema.org. Since authoritative hubs for all six key entities must be created through text and data mining, Chapter 4 surveys relevant research projects that have been conducted at OCLC using advanced algorithms that are required when the information that can be extracted from authority-controlled and other highly structured data is eventually exhausted. Finally, Chapter 5 summarizes the arguments for the approach we have taken and answers questions about how the work will be extended, where the limitations lie, and how linked data models of authoritative hubs will affect future descriptive practice.

1.3.3   A SYSTEMS PERSPECTIVE

OCLC's published linked data markup, the underlying model, and the supporting data resources can be derived only from a complex set of processes involving human analysis, metadata mapping, format conversion, data and text mining, and system-building that is constantly being refined to reveal more and more detail. In its earliest drafts, the model underlying the linked data output may be fully consistent with the current generation of standards and production systems. But Figure 1.9 shows the bigger picture. The processes listed in the box with the title 'WorldCat.org production stream,' shown in green, represent the latest iteration of a decades-old production stream, which maps from non-MARC inputs, normalizes critical fields such as ISBNs, corrects erroneous subject headings, and removes duplicates, producing results that are visible in the user-oriented displays derived from MARC records in WorldCat. The box with the title 'Experimental processes,' shown in blue, lists some of the the two-year-old experimental process flow that generates two outputs: the RDFa markup accessible from WorldCat.org, and a slightly richer RDF dataset with the contents of the entire MARC record that reflects a large, yet-to-be-modeled residue, as well as the results of modeling experiments that are too tentative to be published in a production service or are incompatible with the MARC standard and a record-oriented architecture.

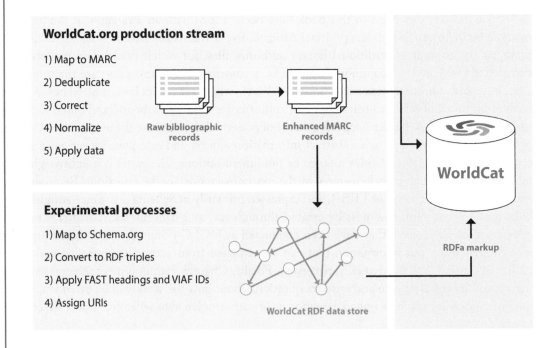

Figure 1.9: Two tracks in the production of WorldCat catalog data.

Other leaders in the library community have described a similar architecture. For example, Gildas Illien, Director of the Bibliographic and Digital Information Department at the Bibliothèque nationale de France, argues in a recent interview (Illien 2013) that libraries cannot afford to wait until their linked data is perfect because they are risking irrelevance by not claiming their rightful place in the Web of Data as early as possible. A better strategy is to demonstrate what is mature and useful now and iteratively improve it as the models are refined and new details are implemented. The initial implementations will be too impoverished to substitute for the legacy systems and will even depend on them, thus generating a need to convert legacy data to the new standards and creating a more complex transitional architecture that enables the old and new systems to coexist. But as they mature, the new systems will become more and more capable of standing alone and will eventually replace the old ones. Illien's remarks were about the linked data experiments being conducted at his institution, but they are an apt description of the evolutionary path that has been defined at OCLC.

The French dataset, first published in 2011 and accessible from `http://data.bnf.fr`, contains links to 200,000 authors, 9,250 creative works, and 170,000 subjects, representing 40% of the references in the French National Catalog, with plans underway to convert the rest. As in WorldCat, the linked data representations are produced by mapping from existing library metadata standards such as MARC and EAD to the corresponding semantics of a new data model that refers to a small set of real-world entities and is capable of generating new output syntaxes such as RDF/XML, RDF/Turtle, and JSON. The effort has already paid off with an award-winning integration of multiple catalogs. It is now possible to issue a single search that delivers consolidated information from the central catalog managed by the library, as well as collections of archival descriptions and digitized objects—resources that once co-existed only as isolated data silos. But as reported by The European Library (TEL 2014a), an even better outcome is that 80% of the hits now originate from the broader Web, bypassing the library's locally maintained search intake systems altogether.

The British Library has also reported a positive outcome from the linked data modeling experiment (BL 2014b). Since 2011, the British National Bibliography has grown into a semantically rich, interconnected network of links to people, places, dates, and subjects in 3.5 million books and serials published in the UK and Ireland since 1950. In 2014, British National Bibliography elicited 2 million transactions per month, has received national accolades, and has been formally incorporated into the British national data infrastructure.

Finally, the project sponsored by the Oslo Public Library has achieved an important milestone, as described in Rekkavik (2014). The linked data version of the Oslo library catalog was developed with a dependency on the legacy production system not unlike OCLC's configuration depicted in Figure 1.9. The experiment has served as a testbed for research projects with goals similar to those pursued at OCLC, which have yielded tools for converting MARC to RDF and descriptions that recognize entities and relationships first defined in the FRBR model of the library catalog. But modeled as linked data, Oslo's next-generation catalog can support a seamless integration of physical and digital resources. The catalog can also bundle descriptions of works in the library collection with related works accessible from the wider Web. Since these innovations cannot be supported in the old standards, the Oslo Public Library has announced the radical step of dropping MARC as a format for resource description. Thus the Oslo linked data experiment has matured to the point that it can stand alone because it now has more functionality than the legacy production system.

1.4   CHAPTER SUMMARY

The successes reported by the Bibliothèque nationale de France, the British Library, and the Oslo Public Library provide a glimpse into the workings of the library of the future, one in which resources in a library's collection are more machine-understandable, are more integrated with the broader Web, and are more consistent with conventions that facilitate consumption by the world's general-purpose search engines, where users are increasingly more likely to discover them. An international consensus is reaching the conclusion that the data architecture for the next-generation library will be built on the data standards and Web protocols discussed in this chapter.

The argument for doing so has multiple layers. The simplest argument is that the new reality is a Web environment in which data standards and communication protocols highlight the need for more structured data with a more broadly understandable meaning derived from richer domain models—enabling machine process to *act* on data that was once merely displayed, to echo the passage quoted at the beginning of this chapter. The library community has no choice but to operate in this environment, both as consumers of the new standards and as contributors who ensure that the world's intellectual heritage is justly represented. Stated more colloquially, this is the external argument for libraries becoming more 'of the Web' and not merely 'on the Web.'

But the internal argument is also compelling. Library standards for resource description date from the dawn of the computer age for civilian applications and have reached the end of their useful life. In the 1960s, a 'Machine-Readable Catalog' (or MARC) record was a major advance over a printed catalog card. But these records are understandable only in the library community—and even there, machine processes are hampered because most of the important assertions encoded as human-readable text, including numeric values such as record identifiers and ISBNs. As Coyle (2012) pointed out, an analysis of more Web-friendly standards such as Dublin Core and ONIX produces a list of milestones that lead to deeper levels of machine understanding because they place a greater premium on converting text to data, data to unambiguous or controlled vocabularies, and records to statements. These milestones can be understood as the preprocessing steps required for publishing linked data, or as inputs to the processes that generate RDF datasets conforming to the criteria listed on Tim Berners-Lee's coffee cup reproduced in Figure 1.5.

Thus there is incremental value in following the path from databases of human-readable records to five-star networks of RDF statements because each milestone promises an outcome that is independently useful. The first is data that is more structured, more normalized, and easier to maintain. A later outcome is data that conforms to an actionable domain model using published standards that renders it understandable outside the context that created it. The ultimate result is data that can be acted upon to produce greater visibility on the Web and syndication by general-purpose search engines.

Many details remain to be worked out in the context of experimentation and research, both at OCLC and elsewhere in the library community. In other words, libraries have just entered the Semantic Web. The focus is on defining descriptive standards and models that conform to them, developing proofs of concept and compelling demonstrations, and generating results that may even exert influence on the still-evolving Web standards. The rest of this book describes some of the next steps toward these goals being undertaken at OCLC. Such ambitions are large, but experiments with linked data have already improved the user experience with library resources and exposed their value more broadly.

CHAPTER 2

Modeling Library Authority Files

2.1 STRINGS AND THINGS

In a keynote speech to a workshop associated with the 2012 LODLAM conference (International Linked Open Data in Libraries, Archives, and Museums), Mia Ridge, chair of the Museums Computer Group and a member of the Executive Council for the Association for Computers in the Humanities, gives a straightforward explanation of the 'Things, not Strings' problem, and hints at a solution:

> "Computers are dumb. Well, they're not as smart as us, anyway. Computers think in strings (and numbers) where people think in 'things.' If I say 'Captain Cook,' we all know I'm talking about a person, and that it's probably the same person as 'James Cook.' The name may immediately evoke dates, concepts around voyages and sailing, exploration or exploitation, locations in both England and Australia …but a computer knows none of that context and by default can only search for the string of characters you've given it. It also doesn't have any idea that 'Captain Cook' and 'James Cook' might be the same person because the words, when treated as a string of characters, are completely different. But by providing a link …that unambiguously identifies 'James Cook,' a computer can 'understand' any reference to Captain Cook that also uses that link." (Ridge 2012)

As shown in Chapter 1, linked data conventions address this problem by encouraging the development of data resources that describe real-world things, and by defining Web standards and protocols that distinguish information objects from real-world objects. Once the solution is implemented, Web documents about Captain Cook will have a resolvable reference to the English explorer instead of the string 'Captain Cook.' Such a reference produces hyperlinks that confer a machine-understandable persistence to real-world objects that transcend a particular text and mimic the human reader's ability to move from text to text, accumulating knowledge about Captain Cook or any other person, place, or thing of interest.

This chapter describes the models for the library authority files most frequently referenced in the linked data markup accessible from WorldCat.org: the Library of Congress Subject Headings, FAST, the Dewey Decimal Classification, and VIAF. In a book that surveys OCLC's contributions to linked data models of library resource description, it is important to highlight the achievements of OCLC researchers who have developed representations for two international standards, as well as the most frequently referenced RDF dataset produced to date by the library community. This outcome depended on groundbreaking work published by the Library of Congress in 2008, as well as the contribution of many other researchers who recognized the primacy of references to real-world objects in bibliographic descriptions and realized that library authority files were designed to achieve the same goal.

Chapter 1 pointed out that authority files were the first data resources maintained by the library community to be modeled as linked data, perhaps because they imply a solution to the 'Things, not Strings' problem. For example, consider the record fragments shown in Figure 2.1. At the top is a human-readable view of a MARC 21 bibliographic record that describes the book *The Journals of Captain James Cook on his Voyages of Discovery*, which was written by a person named James Cook who was born in 1728 and died in 1779. The 'Author' field identifies the author with a formatted string; the same string is repeated as a subject in the 'Subject' field because one of the subjects of James Cook's journal is James Cook himself. This string also appears in the 'Name' field of the record below it, which is based on the MARC Name Authority record for James Cook. The authority record associates this string with a database record identifier, '78091496,' and informs the human reader that the string 'Captain (James) Cook' is a variant form. The bibliographic record shown in Figure 2.1 is said to be 'authority-controlled' because a definitive link has been established between the author or subject in a description of a creative work and a unique record in the MARC Name Authority file. Authority control makes it possible to assemble a collection of resources managed by libraries that are by or about the person named James Cook who lived between 1728 and 1779, excluding authors with the same name who lived in the 19th and 20th centuries and wrote books about law, oil and gas geology, and organic chemistry.

A bibliographic record
Author: Cook, James, 1728-1779
Title: The Journals of Captain James Cook on his Voyages of Discovery
Subject: Voyages around the world
Subject: Cook, James, 1728-1779

An authority record
Record ID: 78091496
Name: Cook, James, 1728-1779
Alternative Name: Cook, Captain (James), 1728-1779

Figure 2.1: A reference to Captain James Cook in hypothetical bibliographic and authority records.

In other words, an authority-controlled MARC record solves part of the problem identified by Mia Ridge. A machine process acting on such records can detect that 'James Cook' and 'Captain Cook' are alternative forms of the same name, and can thus build a context of information extracted from a set of records containing the same disambiguated strings. In the linked data idiom, this outcome is possible because a person has been identified and linked to an authoritative resource, which contains links to other real-world objects.

However, a legacy library authority file does not automatically qualify as a dataset that conforms to the principles of linked data. The key piece of information is not a URI, but a privileged string, or an authorized heading, which serves as an index into a database of authority file records. The heading must be copied verbatim into every record or Web document describing a resource that is by or about Captain James Cook. The link is severed if the heading is misspelled or translated into another language or if it is revised by the authority file editors. Moreover, the link is not globally unique because many national libraries in addition to the Library of Congress maintain authority files that refer to Captain Cook and may define different authorized headings.

In a narrow sense, the conversion of a library authority file to a linked dataset is a technical upgrade that converts records to a graph or network of RDF statements, defines globally unique URIs, and assigns these URIs to the task that is now performed by authorized headings. More broadly, however, the adoption of linked data conventions exerts pressure to change the semantics of the library authority file. As a resource for the library community, the authority file contains information about the strings used to identify titles, authors, and subjects in the published record. To become more broadly useful, however, library authority files must evolve into authoritative hubs about the people, places, and concepts that populate the resources managed by libraries and appear prominently in the broader web of data. The essential insight driving this transformation is that references to the things referenced in a resource description are more valuable, versatile, and reliable than the string values that only human readers can interpret.

2.2   FROM AUTHORITY RECORDS TO RDF TRIPLES

This section describes the evolution from a legacy library standard to the first drafts of library authority files modeled as linked data. It is an intellectual history of sorts, which starts with an the examination of the similarities and differences between strings represented in library authority files such as 'Voyages around the world' and 'Captain James Cook.' From there, the exposition builds up the corresponding linked data models and shows how they are implemented in several of the oldest, largest and most widely used RDF datastores in the library community.

Both strings appear in the hypothetical bibliographic description shown in Figure 2.1, where it is easily inferred that the first is the subject of the book *The Journals of Captain James Cook on his Voyages of Discovery*, and the second is the author. Authoritative sources for the names of subjects and authors include the Library of Congress Subject Headings (or LCSH), the Library of Congress Name Authority File, the Faceted Application of Subject Headings (or FAST), and the Dewey Decimal Classification (or the DDC). They are compatible with the Simple Knowledge Organization System, or SKOS, an RDF meta-vocabulary that was first released in 2004 and promoted to a W3C Recommendation in 2009 (Miles and Bechhofer 2009b). Because SKOS is flexible enough to model thesauri, taxonomies, folksonomies, classification schemes, terminologies, glossaries, and other controlled vocabulary lists, standards experts quickly recognized the overlap with the MARC 21 Format for Authority Data (LC 2014d), the core standard that governs the design of library authority files.

Since the MARC 21 Authority Format is the only permissible carrier for the names, subjects, and classification numbers that qualify as controlled access points in a MARC 21 bibliographic record, the linked datasets containing most of the URIs that are referenced in the RDF statements accessible from WorldCat.org are expressed in SKOS. Nevertheless, the models derived from SKOS have to be supplemented with concepts defined in other Web vocabularies, as we will show.

2.2.1 THE MARC 21 AUTHORITY FORMAT

A pair of MARC 21 authority records anchors the discussion that follows. Figure 2.2 is an excerpt from a Library of Congress Subject Headings topical authority record for the heading 'Food preferences,' and Figure 2.3 is a similarly abridged Library of Congress Name Authority record for the heading 'Twain, Mark, 1835-1910.' In both records, the strings appearing after the $a subfield codes are the literal values that are copied when human catalogers create a MARC 21 bibliographic record. Compound headings such as '$a Nutrition $x Psychological aspects' or '$a Twain, Mark, $d 1835-1910' can be algorithmically converted to human-readable formats, 'Nutrition—psychological aspects' and 'Twain, Mark,—1835–1910.' Figures 2.2 and 2.3 represent abridged versions of the full records; the complete versions can be accessed from id.loc.gov by entering the codes listed in the 001 fields as queries and viewing the results as MARC-XML.

```
010     sh85050304
150 __  $a Food preferences
450 __  $a Food selection
550 __  $w g $a Food habits
550 __  $w g $a Nutrition
550 __  $a Nutrition $x Psychological aspects
550 __  $a Taste
```

Figure 2.2: An abridged Library of Congress topical authority record.

```
010     n79021164
100 __  $a Twain, Mark, $d 1835-1910
400 __  $a Tuèĭn, Mark, $d 1835-1910
400 __  $a Tuwayn, Mārk, $d 1835-1910
500 __  $a Snodgrass, Quintus Curtius, $d 1835-1910
```

Figure 2.3: An abridged Library of Congress name authority record.

The thesaurus structure of the authority record for the topical heading, shown in Figure 2.2, is clearly evident. The 010 field is the Library of Congress Control Number, or LCCN, and can be understood as a unique identifier for the term because a carefully edited authority file maintains a one-to-one relationship between a term and a record. The 150 field contains the authorized form of the term that is licensed to appear in a controlled access field such as 650 in a valid MARC 21 bibliographic record. The 450 field contains an unauthorized equivalent and the 550 fields list related terms, i.e., other authorized headings whose meaning is associated with the one listed in the 150 field. Though 'related' is a slippery term, the presence of the code 'g' in the $w subfield identifies the headings 'Food habits' and 'Nutrition' as having broader meanings than 'Food preferences.' Still, no precise relationship can be inferred for the compound heading 'Nutrition—psychological aspects.'

The Name Authority record shown in Figure 2.3 has essentially the same structure as the topical record, except that the field numbers are multiples of 100 instead of 50, marking this record as a description of a personal name instead of a topic. But the the thesaurus structure is overlaid with features that apply only to personal names and the entities behind them. As in the topical record, the LCCN is available from the 010 field, and the preferred term 'Twain, Mark,— 1835–1910' is listed in the corresponding 1xx field. But the $d subfield lists 'dates associated with the name' (LC 2014d) that are usually interpreted as the person's birth and death dates. Similarly, the 400 fields represent alternative, or unauthorized, forms of the preferred heading. But the alternative headings for personal names are restricted to those rendered in different character sets and transcriptions, such as 'Tuĕĭn, Mark $d 1835-1910,' reflecting the fact that the works of this well-known literary figure have been translated into many languages. Finally, the 500 field, like the corresponding 550 field in the MARC authority record for topical headings, identifies cross-references to other authorized headings related to 'Twain, Mark $d 1835–1910.' Among them are 'Snodgrass, Quintus Curtius $d 1835-1910,' shown in Figure 2.3; as well as 'Conte, Louis de$d 1835-1910,' and 'Clemens, Samuel Longhorne $d 1835-1910,' shown in the complete record available from `http://id.loc.gov/authorities/names/n79021164`. But these headings also have a specialized interpretation applicable only to personal names. Mark Twain, Quintus Curtius Snodgrass, and Louis de Conte are the names of literary personas coined by the true author, Samuel Longhorne Clemens. Some of this subtlety is acknowledged in the 663 field ('Complex See Also Reference-Name'), which contains a note to search for works of this author written under other names.

2.2.2 MARC 21 AUTHORITY RECORDS MODELED IN SKOS

In 2008, a team led by Ed Summers converted the Library of Congress authority files into SKOS RDF/XML (Summers et al. 2008). In May 2009, the Library of Congress made the LCSH vocabulary modeled as SKOS publicly available at `http://id.loc.gov`, and in 2010 published the *LC Thesaurus of Graphic Materials* (Ford 2010).

A SKOS description derived from the Summers project that corresponds to the MARC 21 Authority record in Figure 2.2 is shown in Figure 2.4. The contents are modeled as a skos:Concept, defined in the specification as "an idea or notion; a unit of thought" (Miles and Bechhofer 2009c). The URIs are designed to guarantee uniqueness and persistence by systematically zeroing in on the concept—first identifying the publisher ('loc.gov'), then the class ('authorities') and subclass ('subjects') of the curated resource to which the data belongs, and terminating with the LCCN for an individual record (Miles and Bechhofer 2009b).

```
<http://viaf.org/viaf/50566653/>
<http://id.loc.gov/authorities/subjects/sh85050304>
a skos:Concept ;
    skos:prefLabel "Food preferences" ;
    skos:altLabel "Food selection";
    skos:broader <http://id.loc.gov/authorities/subjects/sh85050275> ;
    skos:broader <http://id.loc.gov/authorities/subjects/sh85093451> ;
    skos:related <http://id.loc.gov/authorities/subjects/sh85093455> ;
    skos:related <http://id.loc.gov/authorities/subjects/sh85132732> .
```

Figure 2.4: An abridged MARC 21 authority record for "Food preferences" as a hypothetical SKOS description.

Since the conversion was done by the Summers team using lexical mappings, the SKOS description presents the same essential content available in the original MARC 21 record. For example, the 150 field is represented as skos:prefLabel and the 450 field is translated to skos:altLabel. The slightly more complex semantics of the 550 field requires a map to skos:related unless a $w field containing the code 'g' is present; in which case, skos:broader is more accurate. As we noted above, 550 fields are authorized Library of Congress terms and would thus have their own URIs in the SKOS representation. Accordingly, the three SKOS 'Concept' classes whose skos:prefLabel values are 'Food habits, Nutrition, Nutrition—Psychological aspects,' and 'Taste' can be accessed from the URIs listed at the bottom of the figure. But since 'Food selection' is an unauthorized heading and does not have a corresponding authority record, no URI can be assigned. As a result, it appears as a string even in the richer SKOS representation.

Figure 2.5 contains the SKOS description corresponding to the MARC 21 Name Authority record for 'Twain, Mark,—1835–1910' shown in Figure 2.3. It is structurally identical to the SKOS description for 'Food preferences.' It is typed as a skos:Concept; the URI is built using the same pattern, except that the data subclass is 'names,' not 'subjects'; and the analogous MARC 100 and 400 fields map to skos:prefLabel and skos:altLabel, with the same consequences for navigation. As in the topical description, the authorized headings that appear in the MARC 500 field have their own authority records from which URIs can be constructed. Thus the URIs listed as objects of the rdfs:seeAlso property resolve to descriptions whose respective skos:prefLabel data values are 'Clemens, Samuel Langhorne, 1835-1910,' 'Snodgrass, Quintus Curtius, 1835-1910,' and 'Conte, Louis de, 1835-1910,' another pseudonym.

```
<http://id.loc.gov/authorities/names/n79021164>
a skos:Concept ;
    skos:prefLabel "Twain, Mark--1835-1910" ;
    skos:altLabel "Tuėĭn, Mark, $d 1835-1910" ;
    skos:altLabel "Tuwayn, Mārk, $d 1835-1910" ;
    rdfs:seeAlso <http://id.loc.gov/authorities/names/n93099439> ;
    rdfs:seeAlso <http://id.loc.gov/authorities/names/n93099461> ;
    rdfs:seeAlso <http://id.loc.gov/authorities/names/no2003079632> .
```

Figure 2.5: Mark Twain described as a skos:Concept.

Mapped to SKOS, the two MARC 21 authority records have the same labels, but the semantics are inescapably different, and the SKOS model is a better fit for the description of topical headings. Since the Library of Congress Subject Headings have a thesaurus-like structure, a controlled string such as 'Food preferences' is not explicitly defined, but it is assumed to be the name of a concept that can be positioned in a larger ontology. In the abridged MARC 21 authority record shown in Figure 2.2, this position is suggested informally through the list of broader and related terms, but the MARC 21 standard also permits a more precise statement with the 053 field, whose value is a code defined in the Library of Congress Classification. As we have seen, these relationships can be expressed naturally and with relatively little loss of information through skos:Concept, skos:prefLabel, skos:altLabel, skos:broader, and skos:related.

The larger context required for interpreting the string 'Twain, Mark,—1835–1910' is not a thesaurus or ontology, however, but a slice of history in which a person named Samuel Longhorne Clemens was born in 1835, published works of literature using the pseudonyms 'Mark Twain,' 'Quintus Curtius Snodgrass,' and 'Louis de Conte,' and died in 1910. To ensure consistency with other authority records, the MARC 21 name authority record declares an authorized form, which is derived from the name of the author listed on the title pages of Mark Twain's published works. As we have seen, the authority record for Mark Twain also contains unauthorized forms of his name, coded with the skos:altLabel property, which are coined by the translators of his novels and essays. But the names listed in the 500 field of the MARC Authority record are coded with rdfs:seeAlso, a property that makes the stronger assertion of referential equivalence: in other words, Mark Twain, Samuel Longhorne Clemens, Qintus Curtius Snodgrass, and Louis de Conte are exactly the same person.

This information can be coded as a SKOS description, but the result is semantically odd. First, the underlying structure is not a set of thesaurus relationships, but a real-world identity with several names, none of which are explicitly labeled as a given name, a pseudonym, or a translated or transcribed name. Second, the controlled string is not literally the attested name of the author, but is instead a complex statement containing the name plus the author's birth and death dates, which are perhaps more reasonably modeled as properties that are crucial for establishing a reference to a person who once lived. Finally, the string 'Twain, Mark,—1835–1910' is modeled as a 'Concept,' not a 'Person' entity. As a result, a description using the SKOS URI defined in Figure 2.5 would state that the well-known author of *Huckleberry Finn* is a skos:Concept whose preferred label is 'Twain, Mark,—1835–1910,' not a person who was born in 1835 and died in 1910 and wrote under the name 'Mark Twain.' Clearly, personal names are richer than a model derived from a that is mapped to SKOS, a shortcoming that requires much of the rest of this chapter to address.

2.2.3 THE FOAF MODEL OF 'PERSON'

The 'Friend of a Friend' (or FOAF) specification was developed in early 2000 as a broad, easy-to-use vocabulary that could be used to describe things on the Web. In the next decade, FOAF evolved into a de facto RDF standard for describing people and social groups; and more broadly, the "basic information about people in present day, historical, cultural heritage and digital library contexts" (Brickley and Miller 2014). From its inception, FOAF was designed to be interoperable with other vocabularies, tools, and services developed for the Semantic Web.

Both FOAF and SKOS can both be used to model important facts about strings such as 'Mark Twain,' but they produce fundamentally different results. The SKOS description shown in Figure 2.5 models Mark Twain as a 'Concept' entity that can be referred to using a variety of strings managed as authorized headings by library catalogers. But the corresponding FOAF description shown in Figure 2.6 models Mark Twain as a 'Person' entity and defines a list of identifying properties such as foaf:name, foaf:birthday, and foaf:gender. As a result of this distinction, the URIs for the two descriptions resolve to different kinds of resources, or real-world things.

```
<http://example.org/foaf/person/50566653/#Mark_Twain>
a foaf:Person ;
    foaf:givenName "Samuel" ;
    foaf:familyName "Clemens" ;
    foaf:birthday "11-30" ;
    foaf:gender "Male" ;
    foaf:name "Mark Twain" ;
    foaf:name "Quintus Curtius Snodgrass" .
```

Figure 2.6: A FOAF description of Mark Twain.

In addition, the identifying information in the FOAF description goes well beyond what can be expressed in the MARC 21 Authority standard and the semantics of the thesaurus that underlies the SKOS specification. Thus the various strings that have been collected in the FOAF description are explicitly identified as names; and the name given at birth, 'Samuel Longhorne Clemens,' is distinguished from pseudonyms and other assigned names. The name strings have also been decoupled from the semantics of the thesaurus underlying the SKOS models, which enforces distinctions among the preferred label 'Twain, Mark, 1835-1910'; the alternative label 'Tuĕin, Mark, 1835-1910'; or a related 'Concept' entity with the preferred label 'Snodgrass, Quinton Curtius, 1835-1910.' Instead, the FOAF description can be enhanced with nicknames, acquaintances, homepages for work and school, thumbnail images, and lists of publications—many of which are, of course, more appropriately applied to living Internet-aware people than to historical figures.

The foaf:focus property shown in Figure 2.7 can be used to associate a resource modeled as skos:Concept to a description of a tangible thing such as foaf:Person. This property was designed to interoperate with descriptions encoded in the SKOS vocabulary "to help indicate specific things (typically people, places, artifacts) that are mentioned in different SKOS schemes (e.g., Thesauri)" (Brickley and Miller 2014). It should be noted that the idea behind the foaf:focus property is not unique to the FOAF vocabulary. The MADS vocabulary has a similar property for associating a description with a real-world object, madsrdf:identifiesRWO, which is modeled as a sub-property of foaf:focus (LC 2012), though this solution is less commonly used.

Figure 2.7: Connecting FOAF and non-FOAF identifiers.

The foaf:focus property is now an established convention for associating skos:Concept descriptions with other entities. It is used in the VIAF model of 'Person' described later in this chapter.

2.2.4   THE LIBRARY OF CONGRESS AUTHORITY FILES

The 2008 publication of the Library of Congress authority files as a collection of 2.6 million RDF triples was the first demonstration of its kind in the library community, a proof of concept of the affinity between library authority files and linked data. The initial project produced a SKOS model that described personal, geographic, and corporate names as well as topical concepts (Summers et al. 2008). This work also demonstrated how controlled vocabularies could be systematically converted into RDF, and realistically stored, disseminated, maintained, and accessed. The result was a procedure that is completely automated and explicit enough to commit to a production schedule. This workflow has been so widely replicated that library data architects now routinely speak of 'SKOSifying,' or converting library authority files to SKOS, as we did at OCLC with the initial RDF version of FAST and the top schedules of the Dewey Decimal Classification.

In the first step, the resource URIs are designed. As we noted above, the URI for a concept managed in a Library of Congress authority file mentions the Library of Congress Control Number, or LCCN, a unique record identifier. An earlier experiment by Harper (2006) had relied on the preferred string label to achieve the same goal, but this design was ultimately replaced with the LCCN because it is more persistent.

The URIs published by the Summers team also implement a recommendation stated in the Cool URIs documentation (Sauermann and Cyganiac 2007) for referring to non-document resources such as 'Concept' and 'Person' entities. The CoolURIs document defines two URI patterns, containing either a 'hash' or a 'slash,' which are interpreted using different HTTP protocols. HTTP servers respond to a 'hash' pattern such as `http://example.com/about#alice` by truncating the URI to a document about Alice, which is delivered in a format requested by the user through content negotiation via HTTP 200, the usual protocol for delivering documents on the Web. By contrast, browsers respond to a URI with a 'slash' preceding the word 'alice,' such as `http://www.example.com/alice`, by redirecting the request to a document about Alice using the HTTP 303 protocol, which signals a reference to a non-deliverable resource and substitutes an authoritative document about it instead. Though the semantics of the second solution are arguably clearer, the Summers team implemented the first solution and appended '#concept' to the end of each LCSH URI, observing that it is more efficient to compute because it does not require a redirection step. The Summers team also defined an 'about' document for each resource instead of using the hash URI to deliver an individual section of a document that describes multiple resources. As a result, their 'hash' solution maintains a one-to-one relationship between documents and the non-document resources they describe, just as the 'slash' solution does, making the differences between the implementations relatively slight.

In subsequent steps, SKOS statements are generated from the legacy source. Though most of the SKOS statements can be produced through lexical relabeling, some need to be assembled through a more complex algorithmic process. For example, many use cases for library authority data require that the language of cataloging be identified, which is available from the 040 field in the MARC 21 Authority Format.

Compound or pre-coordinated headings also require special handling. For example, the heading '$a Nutrition $x Psychological aspects' is converted to the string literal 'Nutrition—psychological aspects' in SKOS RDF and associated with a URI that refers to the psychological aspects of nutrition. This result is possible only if the compound heading has a corresponding LCSH record; otherwise, compound headings would have to resolve to the multiple URIs of their component terms. Since pre-coordinated subject heading schemes use complex, highly productive rules to create phrases that uniquely describe a resource or anticipate a user's search term, the set of attested headings will always be larger than the set of records that define them in the subject heading scheme. We will revisit this issue in the concluding chapter of this book because we view it as an inherent limitation of the linked data paradigm. Nevertheless, post-coordinated subject heading schemes, which contain only individual words or atomic concepts that users combine when searching, may be more a natural fit for the requirements of the linked data architecture.

Though these issues can be addressed through analysis and semi-automated processing, the Summers team also assembled a realistic technology stack that solved the problem at scale. Acknowledging their predecessor (Harper 2006), they demonstrated that large datasets could be produced for persistent, production-quality systems using publicly accessible and lightweight tools. Despite some issues with the backward traversal of XML nodes required to produce full URIs instead of string literals for broader and narrower terms, the conversion processes could be built with XSL stylesheets or Python scripts. On the front end of the system, additional stylesheets implemented content negotiation protocols that produced MARCXML and multiple RDF syntaxes.

2.2.5   THE FACETED APPLICATION OF SUBJECT TERMINOLOGY

The procedures and conventions defined in the Summers project were easily replicated when OCLC developed the RDF model for the collection of vocabularies commonly known as FAST, or the 'Faceted Application of Subject Terminology.' Initiated in 1998, FAST was developed jointly by OCLC and the Library of Congress to provide a post-coordinated version of the Library of Congress Subject Headings (Chan and O'Neill 2010). The redesign has the welcome effect of simplifying the rules for building compound headings, which translates into a low-overhead solution for assigning patron-friendly subject terms to Web resources, archives, journal articles, and other materials that do not usually undergo traditional authority control (Mixter and Childress 2013). As a post-coordinated vocabulary, FAST can also be more easily translated into RDF because authority records already exist for all of its approximately 1.7 million headings.

The FAST vocabulary was originally released as an RDF dataset in December 2011 (OCLC 2011b) and was significantly revised in 2013. The new version incorporates several high-level classes defined in Schema.org, such as 'Topic,' 'Person,' 'Organization,' 'Place,' and 'Event,' which permit the formulation of ordinary-language descriptions that still retain the structure and provenance expected of a controlled vocabulary maintained by the library community.

Figure 2.8 shows a description of the FAST concept 'Food preferences.' Because of its LCSH source, this description consists primarily of the familiar set of preferred and alternative headings and related concepts, modeled using SKOS classes and properties. The schema:sameAs property establishes an equivalence with the corresponding LCSH description. The FAST URI is globally unique, like the LCSH antecedent, because it contains the legacy database record identifier '930981' as a token. But in a deviation from the LCSH design, FAST URIs implement the 'slash' solution described above because they refer to concepts and other non-document resources, which are described in the Generic Document retrieved by the HTTP 303 redirect protocol. The Generic Document itself is simply the set of statements such as those shown in the figure, which can also be delivered through content negotiation as MARC 21, HTML, or RDF/XML. The 'slash' solution was adopted for FAST and OCLC's other linked data models because it can be easily managed by standard RDF utilities.

The FAST RDF is available as a bulk data dump (FAST 2014a), and individual headings can be accessed from a search interface at (FAST 2014b). The URIs for FAST headings are also automatically assigned to bibliographic descriptions accessible from WorldCat.org.

```
<http://id.worldcat.org/fast/930981>
a schema:Topic ;
    dcterms:identifier "930981" ;
    schema:name "Food preferences" ;
    schema:sameAs <http://id.loc.gov/authorities/subjects/sh85050304> ;
    skos:altLabel "Food selection" ;
    skos:inScheme <http://id.worldcat.org/fast/ontology/1.0/#fast> ;
    skos:prefLabel "Food preferences" ;
    skos:related <http://id.worldcat.org/fast/1042187> ;
    skos:related <http://id.worldcat.org/fast/1042226> ;
    skos:related <http://id.worldcat.org/fast/1143475> ;
    skos:related <http://id.worldcat.org/fast/930807> .
```

Figure 2.8: The FAST RDF description of the concept labeled 'Food preferences.'

2.2.6 THE DEWEY DECIMAL CLASSIFICATION

The top-level summaries in 11 languages of the Dewey Decimal Classification, or the DDC, were first published as RDF in 2009. Subsequent enhancements to the RDF dataset were published at http://dewey.info, which established persistent URIs for classes and index terms. In 2012, the DDC RDF was upgraded to include all concepts defined in the full edition, DDC 23. The evolution of the mature model is described in Panzer (2008), Panzer and Zeng (2009), and Mitchell and Panzer (2013). We point out some of the highlights of their analysis here.

Key details of the model are illustrated in Figure 2.10, an image adapted from Panzer (2008). This example shows a fragment of the concept space for the Dewey class corresponding to the number '370.113,' whose preferred English label is 'Vocational education.' The terms displayed against a grey background are reproduced in Figure 2.10 as a set of slightly simplified RDF/Turtle SKOS statements. As in other knowledge organization schemes with a thesaurus-like structure, the DDC concept labeled 'Vocational education' appears in a hierarchy, which contains the class number '370.11,' or 'Education for specific objectives,' as a broader concept and '370.113085,' or 'Parents—vocational education,' as a narrower concept. In addition, 'Vocational education' is associated with concepts defined in other Dewey class hierarchies through entries in the Dewey Relative Index, such as 'Vocational schools,' the English-language preferred label for the class number '373.24.' LCSH concepts such as 'Career education—United States' are also mapped to the Dewey class '370.11' through a separate editorial process. These relationships are modeled using the properties skos:prefLabel, skos:broader, skos:narrower, and skos:related. In addition, the DDC model for 'Vocational education' includes the property skos:notation to identify the language-independent class number '370.11.'

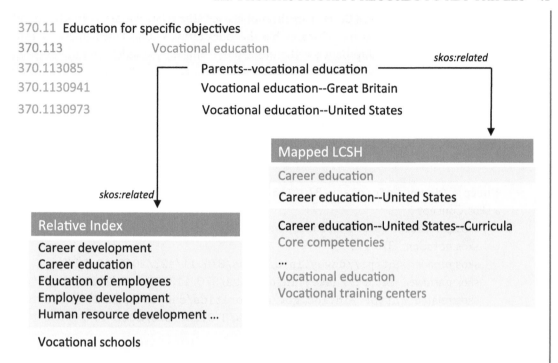

Figure 2.9: The concept space for the DDC class number 370.113. Adapted from Panzer (2008).

Figure 2.10 also shows that Dewey classes are modeled using skos:Concept with a variation of the resolution semantics described in Summers et al. (2008). The URI is built from six kinds of tokens: the name of the project, 'dewey.info'; the name of an object defined in the Dewey metalanguage, such as 'class,' as in this example—or 'schedule,' 'index,' 'table,' or 'summary'; the name of the corresponding published DDC edition, 'e23'; a date stamp for the extracted data, '2012-10-24'; the word 'about,' labeling this set of statements as a description of a non-document resource; and a language token, 'en,' which identifies this set of statements as an English-language description of the concept.

The URI structure implies that the terms defined in the DDC metalanguage overlap only partially with SKOS, raising many problems for the definition of an RDF model. One problem is that SKOS cannot express the meaning of the DDC 'centered entry,' as Panzer and Zeng (2009) argue. For example, the notation 'T2–485' represents 'Sweden' and can be modeled as a skos:Concept, while the centered entry 'T2 - 486 - T2 - 488' encompasses the geographical subdivisions of Sweden. The centered entry is subordinate to 'Sweden' and a parent to the concepts below it—i.e., the names of the individual provinces. But the centered entry is not formally defined and acts only as a placeholder for a span of numbers. As a result, no URI can be assigned. Panzer and Zeng considered modeling the centered entry as a skos:Collection, but this solution is problematic because skos:Collection and skos:Concept are disjoint classes. The relative index is another problem. For example, the Dewey class '616 Diseases' has the index terms 'Clinical medicine' and 'Internal medicine,' but the relationship between the index terms and the class definition is unspecified. In the solution proposed by Panzer and Zeng, each DDC class and index term is represented as a skos:Concept. 'Clinical medicine' is then associated with the Dewey class '616 Diseases' via the property skos:hasIndexTerm, a subproperty of skos:CloseMatch. These two problems show that SKOS is an imperfect fit for a sophisticated classification scheme. As the name implies, SKOS was developed as a 'Simple' ontology and was not designed to for complex vocabularies or thesauri.

```
<http://dewey.info/class/370.113/e23/2012-10-24/about/en>
a skos:Concept ;
    skos:prefLabel "Vocational education" ;
    skos:notation "370.113" ;
    skos:broader <http://dewey.info/class/370.11/e23/2012-10-24/> ;
    skos:narrower <http://dewey.info/class/370.113085/e23/2012-10-24/> ;
    skos:related <http://id.loc.gov/authorities/subjects/sh2008100128> ;
    skos:related <http://dewey.info/class/373.246/e23/2012-10-24/> .
```

Figure 2.10: RDF/Turtle statements for a fragment of the DDC concept 370.113.

Because of the mismatch between the SKOS and DDC semantics, the RDF model of the DDC is not as rich as the print version, but it is superior in other respects. For example, the SKOS dataset can be queried through a SPARQL endpoint (DDC 2014). Since the publication of the RDF dataset, the Dewey team has been investigating ways to enhance the dataset and make it more useful to users. One improvement proposed by Mitchell and Panzer (2013) is a set of links from the Dewey geographical terms to GeoNames. They recommend the use of foaf:focus, a FOAF property discussed in the next section of this chapter, to connect a skos:Concept such as 'T2–485' to the GeoNames entity for Sweden (which is classified as a geonames:Feature). As the authors point out, the *New York Times* recently published their data as RDF and connected their geographical terms to GeoNames. If the same change were applied to the DDC, articles published with *New York Times* headings could be discoverable through Dewey classes.

The DDC model demonstrates that SKOS is not rich enough to capture all of the information in a library authority file, even when the focus is restricted to models of topical subject headings. Although SKOS lacks some important granularity, the conversion process first defined by the Summers team is both explicit and simple enough that nearly anyone with self-taught scripting skills and access to a MARC 21-compliant authority file can conduct experiments capable of producing mature results. The most important outcome of this work is that it is now technically feasible to record the subject of a book by embedding a URI instead of the literal string, thus sidestepping the problems with maintenance and data quality mentioned in the opening paragraphs of this chapter.

2.2.7   SUMMARY: FIRST-GENERATION RDF MODELS OF LIBRARY AUTHORITY FILES

The most important outcome of the projects described in this section is a set of first-draft RDF datasets generated from legacy library authority files. Because of the close fit between the MARC Authority format and the SKOS ontology, the conversion process is well-understood and mechanical, if certain requirements are met: the source dataset has a thesaurus-like structure, there is a one-to-one relationship between a concept definition and a database record, and the record has a persistent identifier that can be repurposed into a globally unique URI. But only the largest and most widely used library authority files have been converted to RDF. Still missing are vocabularies maintained by most of the world's national libraries, as well as vocabularies developed for many scholarly disciplines and types of specialized materials.

The new format offers the promise that library authorities can be integrated more deeply with the broader Web, while raising questions about the appropriateness of the thesaurus model for referents that are physical or tangible objects in the real world. For example, the model of a person in an 'author' relationship to a creative work is still unsettled, though this connection should be at the very center of a model of library resource description. As the discussion has shown, the conversion of a name authority record from MARC to SKOS has simply moved the problems in the original specification to the new format.

In particular, SKOS is still a model of curated strings. When the object of description is a person and the source is a MARC authority record, birth and death dates are among those strings, though they are more naturally expressed as properties defined in a 'Person' class. This problem is addressed in FOAF, though only partially, because the ontology does not define a death date. In addition, FOAF does not support a well-rounded description of a person with multiple identities or personas. Of course, Samuel Longhorne Clemens might be viewed as an outlier in the literary canon because he wrote under multiple pseudonyms. But an actionable model of the 'Person' entity should allow for the possibility of personas with multiple names to account for a child with a nickname, a blogger with an alias, an employee with an ID, or a researcher with a standard name identifier. In the next section, this issue is revisited when we discuss the model of 'Person' in VIAF.

2.3   THE VIRTUAL INTERNATIONAL AUTHORITY FILE

The Virtual International Authority File, or VIAF, merges the data maintained in the most widely used library authority files and makes the results available to a worldwide audience of data consumers. The project was motivated by the concern that multiple national libraries maintain authorized headings for the same individuals attested in the published record, such as 'Mark Twain,' but produce results that are either redundant or irreconcilably different. Thus VIAF was designed to reduce the cost of library authority control through collaborative effort, creating more reliable links to, from, and among library resources.

Working initially with the Deutsche Nationalbibliothek and the Library of Congress, OCLC published the first proof-of-concept prototype in 1998 and since 2011 has offered VIAF as a hosted service. Since 2003, VIAF has been managed as an international consortium. In July 2014, the VIAF Consortium had participants from 29 countries, representing 24 national libraries and 14 other agencies. At that time, the VIAF database contained 35 million personal names, over 5 million corporate names, nearly a half million geographic names, and over two million standardized or uniform titles, or names of creative works (OCLC 2014a). This collection was built from nearly 45 million authority records, from which OCLC's aggregation process established over 30 cross-references (Hickey 2013).

VIAF was originally developed as a database of library authority files derived from the MARC Authority standard. But in 2006, OCLC researchers began to publish some of the data as RDF. The result was a dataset containing 9.5 million entities (Hickey 2009), which has continued to grow. The VIAF RDF dataset is downloaded approximately 150 times per week and is a commonly cited RDF dataset.

Since its initial release, the VIAF RDF dataset has undergone many updates and modifications that align it more closely with the standards and best practices emerging from the linked data community. Some of the changes have been technical or stylistic, but the most fundamental change is the same one that affected the other models of library authority files we have surveyed so far in this chapter. Like FAST—and to some extent, the Library of Congress authority files—the current RDF version of VIAF is now less about curated strings for the names of concepts and more about the real-world entities whose importance has been recognized by librarianship. As in the earlier examples, the evolving RDF model for VIAF is best understood by first examining its MARC-based predecessor.

2.3.1   THE VIAF DATABASE RECORD STRUCTURE

A user who searches for 'Mark Twain' in http://viaf.org views a results list containing, among other things, a link to a description of the author of *The Adventures of Huckleberry Finn* and *Tom Sawyer*, as well as links to Samuel Longhorne Clemens, Quintius Snodgrass, and descriptions of the archives, collections, and societies that are named in Twain's honor.

Figure 2.11 shows a partial view of the VIAF description for Mark Twain the author. The first segment lists the VIAF identifier '50566653'—whose meaning has evolved, in a similar way to the Library of Congress Control Number discussed earlier in this chapter.

In the traditional MARC 21–oriented view visible from VIAF.org, the VIAF identifier can be interpreted as a record number for the description of Mark Twain the author. But as the key component of the URI http://viaf.org/viaf/50566653, the VIAF identifier points to the unique real-world individual, as we will explain below. The first section also lists preferred forms of Mark Twain's name that have been extracted from authority files, whose diverse origins are

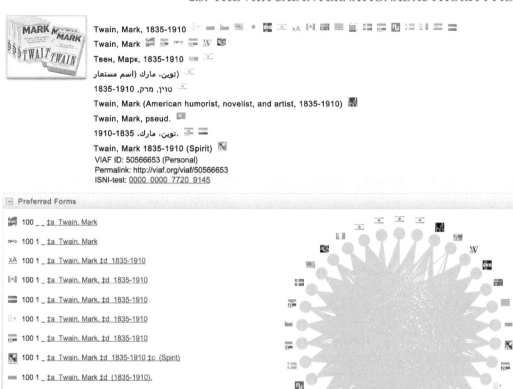

Figure 2.11: An excerpt from the VIAF description for Mark Twain.

represented visually by a set of icons. The complete list of preferred forms is shown in the second segment and the interconnections that have been computed by the VIAF clustering algorithms are depicted in the starburst pattern on the right. Starbursts representing internationally important historical figures such as Mark Twain are especially dense because their works are widely translated and held in libraries all over the world. Other segments not shown in Figure 2.11 link to VIAF entries for alternate and related forms of the name; uniform titles, about which we will have more to say later in this section and in Chapters 3 and 4; alternate views of the record, which we discuss below; as well as countries of publication, related names, co-authors, publishers, and publication statistics.

The last segment preserves the revision history of the VIAF identifier. Since the contents of the record are assembled from inputs provided by third parties, the identity may not be stable if it is computed from sparse or noisy data. The clustering algorithms are tuned to make conservative decisions and may produce multiple VIAF identifiers for the same individual in these circumstances, which can be merged when more data becomes available. This segment makes it possible for a human or machine process to follow the path from a deprecated identifier to the current one.

In the 'Record Views' section, a click on the link labeled 'MARC 21' reveals a record containing elements from the MARC 21 bibliographic and authority standards, as well as some locally defined fields. Such a custom design is necessary, because no existing standard adequately represents the semantics of an aggregated authority file. WorldCat cataloging data is mined to produce a 'Derived Authority,' which contains lists of publications by and about the person or entity of interest, co-authors, important dates and geographic locations, and other inputs to an algorithm that clusters data describing a unique identity. The 'Derived Authority' is combined with the controlled strings and lifespan dates obtained from the aggregated authority records to produce the 'Processed Authority,' which is the record accessible from the VIAF interface. This data flow is depicted schematically in Figure 2.12.

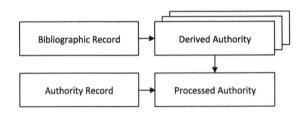

Figure 2.12: Data flow for the construction of a VIAF record. Adapted from Hickey (2013)).

Figure 2.13 shows an excerpt of the record reconstructed from the MARC-XML view. Aside from two custom-defined fields—the 910, which contains the title of one of Mark Twain's books, and the 370 field, which mentions the name of an important geographic location—the record resembles a MARC 21 Authority record, with one important deviation. As in the corresponding MARC 21 Authority record fragment reproduced in Figure 2.3, the 400 field represents an alternate form of the heading and the 500 field cites the preferred form of a related heading. The $2 fields contain codes that identify data contributors: the Library of Congress (LC); the Deutsche Nationalbibliothek (DNB); the Russian State Library (RSL); the National Library of Australia (NLA); and many others listed in the full version of the record.

But the preferred headings are coded as 700 fields instead of 100 fields because the MARC 21 Authority standard permits multiple 700 fields but only a single 100 field per record. The semantics of the 700 field in the VIAF Derived Authority otherwise conforms to the standard. The $0 subfield lists the unique identifier assigned to the record in the source authority file for which the string listed in the $a subfield is the preferred label. The identifier is preceded by a two-

```
700 __   $a Twain, Mark, $d 1835-1910 $0 (LC)n79021164
700 __   $a Twain, Mark, $d 1835-1910 $0 (NLA)000035028957
700 __   $a Твен, Марк, $d 1835-1910 $0 (RSL)nafpn-000083946
370 __   $a Hannibal, Mo. $0 (LC)n82211785
400 __   $a Tuĕin, Mark, $d 1835-1910 $2 NLA $2 LC
500 __   $a Snodgrass, Quintus Curtius, $d 1835-1910 $2 NLA $2 LC
910 __   $a Adventures of Huckleberry Finn $2 LC
```

Figure 2.13: An excerpt from the VIAF record for Mark Twain; VIAF ID 50566653.

or three-letter acronym for the name of the source authority, a mnemonic for the human reader or software process.

This example provides a glimpse of the large and rich VIAF database record structure, which is designed to merge library authority files developed by different national libraries into a single hub of authoritative information expressed in multiple languages and character sets. A clustering algorithm permits a software process to associate the VIAF identifier '50566653' with the two other identifiers shown in Figure 2.13: '000035028957' and 'nafpn-000083946,' the identifiers defined by the National Library of Australia and the Russian State Library. A human reader can make the stronger inference that all three identifiers refer to the same unique real-world individual, but a more sophisticated data model is required before a machine process can do the same.

2.3.2   THE VIAF MODEL OF 'PERSON'

In VIAF, much of the RDF model is populated with data elements that map from the MARC 21 Authority specification to SKOS. But it is enhanced with an explicit reference to the world beyond the text. 'Person' was originally modeled in FOAF, but the RDF markup on VIAF was republished using the semantically similar schema:Person in September 2014.

Figure 2.14 shows an RDF/Turtle version of the relevant fields of the pseudo-MARC 21 record corresponding to Figure 2.13. As in the earlier example, Figure 2.14 is a simplified excerpt designed to aid exposition. The complete description is much larger and can be viewed as RDF/XML in the 'Record Views' section of the relevant VIAF record. The core concept is a schema:Person with the VIAF identifier '50566653.' Accordingly, the URI http://viaf.org/viaf/50566653 resolves with the HTTP 303 redirect, delivering an authoritative, content-negotiable document surrogate for the person who wrote works of literature under the name 'Mark Twain.'

Many of the statements in the first block describe Mark Twain using properties from Schema.org, converting the controlled string imported from a library authority file source to a structured format that identifies the first and last names and lifespan dates. The owl:sameAs statement establishes a referential equivalence between the people named 'Mark Twain' described in

```
<http://viaf.org/viaf/50566653/>
a schema:Person ;
    schema:familyName "Twain" ;
    schema:givenName "Mark" ;
    schema:birthDate "1835" ;
    schema:deathDate "1910" ;
    owl:sameAs <http://dbpedia.org/resource/Mark_Twain> ;
    schema:alternateName "Conte, Louis de" ;
    schema:alternateName "Snodgrass, Quintus Curtius" ;
    rdfs:seeAlso <http://viaf.org/viaf/178806136> .

<http://viaf.org/viaf/sourceID/LC%7Cn++79021164#skos:Concept>
a skos:Concept ;
    skos:inScheme <http://viaf.org/authorityScheme/LC> ;
    skos:prefLabel "Twain, Mark, 1835-1910" ;
    skos:altLabel "Make Teviin, 1835-1910" ;
    skos:altLabel "Твен, Марк, 1835-1910" ;
    skos:exactMatch <http://id.loc.gov/authorities/names/n79021164> ;
    foaf:focus <http://viaf.org/viaf/50566653> .

<http://viaf.org/viaf/sourceID/NLA%7C000035028957#skos:Concept>
a skos:Concept ;
    skos:inScheme <http://viaf.org/authorityScheme/NLA> ;
    skos:prefLabel "Twain, Mark, 1835-1910" ;
    skos:altLabel "Make Tuwen, 1835-1910" ;
    foaf:focus <http://viaf.org/viaf/50566653> .

<http://viaf.org/viaf/sourceID/RSL%7Cnafpn-000083946#skos:Concept>
a skos:Concept ;
    skos:inScheme <http://viaf.org/authorityScheme/RSL> ;
    skos:prefLabel "Твен, Марк, 1835-1910" ;
    skos:altLabel "Клеменс, СамузльЛангхорн 1835-1910" ;
    foaf:focus <http://viaf.org/viaf/50566653> .
```

Figure 2.14: An RDF/Turtle excerpt of the VIAF description of Mark Twain; ID: 50566653.

VIAF and DBpedia, an RDF-encoded structured dataset extracted from Wikipedia. The statements with the schema:alternateName property contain the translated and transliterated forms of the name 'Mark Twain.' The rdfs:seeAlso statement establishes another referential identity: between the person named Mark Twain that the VIAF description is about, and the person with the same name who is described in other library authority files as the author of *Huckleberry Finn*.

Unfortunately, the relationships between the real-world person given the name 'Samuel Clemens' at birth and his adult identities are not yet adequately captured. Such gaps are addressable in BiblioGraph (BGN 2014a), an extension vocabulary for Schema.org designed to meet the needs of librarians, library systems vendors, and publishers, which is discussed in more detail in Chapter 3. The problem can be solved by defining the BiblioGraph term bgn:isPseudonymOf, which is used in a description of Mark Twain to create the machine-understandable statement 'Mark Twain is a pseudonym of Samuel Longhorne Clemens.' Conversely, bgn:hasPseudonym could be used to state that Samuel Longhorne Clemens has the pseudonymn 'Mark Twain.' These terms are definable as additional properties for the schema:Person class. These terms have not been published in BiblioGraph, however, because the model of a literary persona is still being developed.

The remaining RDF statements in Figure 2.14 encode descriptions of concepts modeled as skos:Concept extracted from the authority files that comprise the VIAF aggregation. They have the same internal structure. First, an entity represented in the authority file is associated with a URI. If the source authority file has been modeled as RDF by a recognized maintenance agency, the block contains a skos:exactMatch statement with a URI from the source. Of the three descriptions listed in Figure 2.14, only the concept derived from a Library of Congress source has a native URI. Otherwise, the process stream managed at OCLC generates a conditional RDF model containing URIs with a 'VIAF' token. Each locally constructed URI also contains a token representing an acronym for the source authority, such as 'NLA' for the National Library of Australia. Finally, each URI contains the unique number assigned to the concept in the source database record, such as the RSL identifier 'nafpn-000083946.' The skos:inScheme statement refers the reader or a machine process to more information about the authority file. A foaf:focus statement associates the description with Mark Twain, the real-world person referenced by the VIAF identifier '50566653.' Finally, the statements containing the skos:prefLabel and skos:altLabel can be assigned the same interpretation as the corresponding statements in Figure 2.5: the preferred label represents a controlled string and the alternative label is an uncontrolled variant, according to the agency that controls the record.

These relationships are shown as a hub-and-spoke configuration in Figure 2.15. At the center is the core entity schema:Person, and on the periphery is a set of descriptions obtained from the aggregated authority files.

In Figure 2.15, the focal point is a schema:Person. But in the initial version of the VIAF RDF model, the class viaf:NameAuthorityCluster was defined as the hub instead, reflecting the earlier interpretation of VIAF as an aggregate of strings. Figure 2.16 shows the most important details of this model. The grayed-out elements describe the form and provenance of the source strings

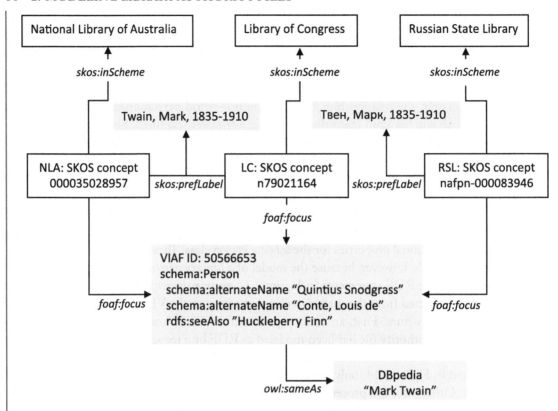

Figure 2.15: A schematic view of the VIAF resource description model.

in essentially the same terms as the current version. The main difference is that the name strings associated with 'Person' entities were modeled in the viaf:NameAuthorityCluster class, while other identifying information was modeled in the foaf:Person class, which were associated through the foaf:focus property.

Figure 2.16: An earlier version of VIAF modeled as a viaf:NameAuthorityCluster.

Though the links between the skos:Concept layer and the viaf:NameAuthorityCluster are arguably more straightforward in this model, the design was abandoned. One problem was that viaf:NameAuthorityCluster was an opaque artificial construct with no published definition or properties, yet it was the referent of the canonical VIAF URI, `http://viaf.org/viaf/xxxxx`. But it could refer only to "an accumulation of labels" (Young 2011), and not directly to a person, thus motivating the need for a separate foaf:Person class. Even so, the statements containing skos:prefLabel were available only in the source authority descriptions, not in the hub, requiring a machine process to traverse the RDF graph to locate them. Another problem was that the collection of authorized strings across multiple files made it necessary to describe relationships among the underlying concepts separately from the string labels for them, a distinction captured in the FRSAD concepts 'Thema' and 'Nomen' (Zeng, Zumer, and Salaba 2010). But a model with this detail required an additional class, skosxl:Labels (Miles and Bechhofer 2009a), an extra URI pattern that differentiated the VIAF identifier from the string label, and a retrospective conversion that was not guaranteed to be reliable.

In the end, the effort required to align VIAF with the FRSAD model was deemed impractical for everyday use. As a result of the revision of the previous model to the current one, the referent for the canonical VIAF identifier changed from an artificial construct to a real-world object. This was a radical shift that positioned VIAF to evolve into an authoritative hub of data—primarily about people, but also about a small number of places, organizations, and works—which is managed by the library community in a format that can be consumed by the broader Web. The change marked a bold departure from legacy library standards, a change that was bound to happen, because the MARC 21 Format for Authority Data was never a good fit for the semantics of a trans-national aggregation.

2.3.3   A NOTE ABOUT UNIFORM TITLES

The RDF model for VIAF is the most mature and comprehensive for personal names and the people behind them. But descriptions of organizations, geographic features and locations, creative works are also accessible by choosing the appropriate item from the menu labeled 'Select Field' on the VIAF search interface. Anticipating the subject of the next chapter, we note here that the description of creative works is the focus of much experimentation by OCLC researchers. Works usually make their appearance in VIAF as the so-called 'uniform titles' defined in MARC authority files and referenced in bibliographic records (LC 2014a).

A MARC-like representation of a description of *Huckleberry Finn* is shown in Figure 2.17. It is similar to the corresponding description of Mark Twain shown in Figure 2.14 because the input fields consist primarily of author-title pairs coded as MARC 700 and 400 fields. But descriptions of 'Work' and 'Person' entities are different because a Work description has a 240 'Uniform Title' field and the $t subfields of the 400 and 700 fields contain string variants of a single title, not multiple titles.

```
240 $a Twain, Mark $d 1835-1910 $t The Adventures of Huckleberry Finn $0 (BNF) 12036903
700 $a Twain, Mark $d 1835-1910 $t Adventures of Huckleberry Finn $0 (NLA) 000035028959
700 $a Twain, Mark $d 1835-1910 $t Adventures of Huckleberry Finn $0 (LC) n 79132705
700 $a Twain, Mark $d 1835-1910 $t Adventures of Huckleberry Finn (Tom Sawyer's comrade)
700 $a Twain, Mark $d 1835-1910 $t Adventures of Huckleberry Finn (Tom Sawyer's companion)
```

Figure 2.17: An excerpt from the VIAF record for Huckleberry Finn; VIAF ID 178806136.

An excerpt from the corresponding RDF/Turtle representation is shown in Figure 2.18. Like the description of Mark Twain shown in Figure 2.14, the top-level referent is explicitly identified as a real-world object defined in Schema.org. Here it is a schema:CreativeWork instead of a schema:Person, with properties such as schema:name, schema:alternateName, schema:author, and schema:inLanguage.

```
<http://viaf.org/viaf/178806136>
a schema:CreativeWork ;
    schema:name "The Adventures of Huckleberry Finn" ;
    schema:alternateName "Adventures of Huckleberry Finn" ;
    schema:author <http://viaf.org/viaf/50566652> ; # Mark Twain
    schema:inLanguage "English" .

<http://viaf.org/viaf/307640027>
a schema:CreativeWork ;
    schema:name "Adventures of Huckleberry Finn" ;
    schema:inLanguage "Afrikaans" ;
    bgn:translationOfWork <http://viaf.org/viaf/178806136> .
```

Figure 2.18: An RDF/Turtle description of Huckleberry Finn; VIAF ID 178806136.

The second block of RDF statements shows one result from the Multilingual WorldCat project (Gatenby 2013), about which we have more to say in Chapter 3. It describes a Work with the VIAF identifier '307640027' representing the Afrikaans translation of Huckleberry Finn, which has the bgn:translationOfWork relationship to the English-language original. The new property is defined in BiblioGraph (BGN 2014a), OCLC's extension vocabulary for Schema.org. By mining WorldCat for evidence of translations such as this one, we can expand the scope and depth of Work descriptions in VIAF well beyond the baseline contributed by human catalogers. In the process, we demonstrate the value of a model whose core concept is no longer an aggregation of controlled strings, but a set of references to things in the world such as 'Person' and 'Work' entities.

2.4   CHAPTER SUMMARY

Authority files were originally developed to make it easier for library patrons to find books by title, author, or subject. The primary use case for library authority files created a need to manage sets of specially formatted strings defined as authorized headings, embedding them in database records containing related authorized headings and unauthorized variants. When the heading is a common noun — or, more technically, a topical subject heading — such as 'democracy' or 'cooking,' the collection of formatted strings defined by the MARC Authority standard resembles a thesaurus, in which the authorized heading is the most common or stable name of a concept, while the less commonly attested unauthorized variants may have recognizable relationships to the authorized heading such as 'Broader-than' and 'Narrower-than.' As we have seen, the bridge from the record-based formats of traditional authority files to a web of machine-processable statements modeled as linked data can be easily crossed, perhaps because models for library authority files encode some of the most important prerequisites, such as persistent identifiers and implicit references to world outside collections of strings. Semantic Web models such as SKOS express nearly everything that can be declared in the old data structures when the term is a topical heading.

We have also argued that controlled strings representing the names of people require a different model that is not adequately expressed in traditional library authority standards. Establishing a link between a proper noun and a unique identity is fundamentally a problem about naming and reference, not the placement of a concept definition in a thesaurus. The problem is addressed through a richer model that defines characteristics of real-world objects and is realized through a Web protocol that delivers an authoritative document as a stand-in for the object itself. This solution makes it possible to state an obvious conclusion about proper names in library authority files: the model that underlies such resources is not wrong, but incomplete, and the solution we have described is a realistic way of extending it.

The problem can be illustrated with personal names, but the same arguments apply to corporate and geographic names. In the case of geographic names, the argument that library authority files can be extended through references to resources maintained by third parties is even stronger because the real-world referents can be even more clearly secured through a reference to geospatial coordinates and other properties that have been modeled in GeoNames. Corporate names present unique modeling challenges that have not yet been addressed by librarians or modeling experts in the linked data community. For example, a model of naming and reference for corporate entities requires time and space dimensions because companies merge, split, change their names, and move around. This is a topic for future work, but we identify some of the issues in our discussion of publisher names in MARC 21 records in Chapter 4.

Once these efforts achieve maturity, however, they raise issues about the intended scope and purpose of the redesigned authority files. As linked data, descriptions of real-world objects derived from library authority files are modeled in a format that can be broadcast to the Web, where they can be leveraged more widely to construct trusted assertions about creative works, authorship, and the vocabulary of topics and subjects. In the larger context of the Web of Data, they can be augmented with links to authoritative datasets managed by third parties, such as Geonames and Wikipedia, as we have pointed out. But library authority control remains a technical specialty of librarianship, managed by established governance structures to advance the goal of improving indexes of library catalogs, primarily for the resources types defined for MARC: books, computer files, maps, archives and other mixed materials, visual materials, music, and serials. Do the enhanced RDF datasets generated from library authority files serve the same purpose? And if not, what purpose do they serve?

One answer is that the redesigned library authority files present an opportunity to expand the evidence for the current model by increasing the connectivity between library authority files and other sources of vetted information about the authors of creative works. For example, Klein and Kyrios (2013), acting as registered Wikipedians, have devised an algorithm called VIAFbot, which has produced several hundred thousand links from VIAF to Wikipedia, primarily from English-language biographies of famous authors. In a separate process, the VIAF links are propagated to non-English versions of Wikipedia via Wikidata (Klein 2013). At the conclusion of their study, Klein and Kyrios point out the mutual benefits of this effort:

> "The VIAFbot initiative has connected library authority data with hundreds of thousands of pages on one of the world's most popular websites, increasing the visibility and availability of that data and, by extension, libraries as an institution. The positive reception to the project at Wikipedia affirms the strength of libraries in performing authority control and proves the utility of this work in the era of linked data. The project offers a blueprint for similar efforts to integrate library data with Wikipedia and, perhaps even more importantly, has built good will for the library community with Wikipedia. At a time when many libraries worry about keeping up with information in a digital world, collaborations like this one offer an exciting glimpse of what libraries can still do to help connection their users with high-quality information resources." (Klein and Kyrios 2013)

But a more far-reaching answer is that the transformation from a collection of human-readable database records to a network of machine-processable statements presents a unique opportunity to expand the scope of the model of library resource description devoted to the definition of relationships among creative works, subjects, and the agents involved in their creation or management. For example, in addition to statements such as 'Mark Twain is the author of *Huckleberry Finn*,' or '*The Omnivore's Dilemma* is about food preferences,' academic librarians are also responding to the pressure to make unambiguous, machine-processable statements that encode such assertions as as 'Lonnie Thompson is a professor at Ohio State University and is an expert on global warming.' 'Tim Berners-Lee is an author of The Semantic Web So Far.' and 'Edessa is the capital of Orshoene.' These statements illustrate the need to identify relationships between authors and their areas of expertise in the larger task of describing the intellectual capital of a particular university, to apply authority control to journal articles, and to manage the names important to scholarly inquiry regardless of whether they are the subjects of published works. This landscape is rapidly evolving (Smith-Yoshimura 2013; Smith-Yoshimura et al. 2014), and governed by imperatives that are sometimes at odds with the traditional practice of library authority control (Smith-Yoshimura and Michelson 2013).

Thus it is not yet clear that the results of this effort will always be applied to existing authority files. An alternative is an authoritative hub defining 'Person' and other entities managed with goals and descriptive practices that only partially overlap with those of traditional library authority control . Regardless of how these changes are recorded, however, the wider Web can only be enriched by the datasets endorsed by libraries. The outcome is an argument in favor of the models developed in the linked data paradigm, and a starting point for the design of hubs for other key entities that are referenced in descriptions of library resources.

CHAPTER 3

Modeling and Discovering Creative Works

3.1 LIBRARY CATALOGING AND LINKED DATA

So far, the discussion has focused on the assertions about people, places, organizations, and concepts associated with the description of *The Adventures of Huckleberry Finn*, *Hamlet*, and *American Guerrilla*, and many other creative works mentioned in the previous pages, but it has omitted the most important detail of all. What, exactly, *is* a creative work? We can presume that descriptions excerpted from WorldCat cataloging data, library catalogs, or bookseller websites such as Amazon.com are comprehensible to casual readers because they refer to objects that can be experienced in some fashion, by searching for, borrowing, buying, reading, skimming, studying, holding, or accessing via a link on a website. They are real-world objects. The view of the information consumer might also embrace the understanding that these objects were brought into being through a creative process of some sort, were manufactured into something physical or tangible, and acquired by a library, which makes them available for access. The same person probably knows that libraries have other things besides books, so a description in a library catalog can also refer to DVDs, e-books, music recordings, maps, photographs, and magazines—but is unlikely to be about electronics or kitchen gadgets. All of these statements are part of a mental model of what libraries are for, a cultural understanding that is more sophisticated than it appears, because a similar model of what Amazon.com is about would resemble the library model in some respects, but differ in others. For example, a customer's model of Amazon would encode the knowledge that a book can be bought if it cannot be found in a library and that household items can be obtained from one source but not the other.

Chapter 1 pointed out that the description of creative works represents the leading edge of linked data modeling efforts in the library community. To make progress, three large problems must be addressed. First, creative works are ontologically complex. On the one hand, a creative work is a thought, an idea, a notion, or a search query; but it is also the physical or tangible object that is eventually obtained through the search. To model this reality, OCLC's experiments mention all six of the key entities described in this book—People, Places, Organizations, Concepts, Works, and Objects—placing special emphasis on the last two. Another problem is that there is no ready-made or easily adaptable descriptive standard. In the library community, legacy standards are large and text-heavy, while the linked data models are still too immature to support the day-to-day activities in a library. Elsewhere on the Web, Schema.org is more established, but the model of schema:CreativeWork is richly detailed only for resources that are produced and traded through the publisher supply chain.

The final problem is that a linked data model of creative works threatens to be more disruptive to existing descriptive practice in the library community, because it falls into the divide between authority control and cataloging. As we argued in Chapter 2, a linked data representation of a library authority file can be viewed as a mostly invisible technical upgrade that establishes references to the real-world objects they describe through globally unique URIs instead of formatted text strings. But the cataloging workflow is more complex. One task is name and subject analysis, which is already taking advantage of the improved authority files produced from the linked data experiments. Another is the preparation of the item in hand for access by affixing a spine label or assigning a URL and creating a description that lists details such as the author and contributors, physical features, and multiple forms of the title. But the execution of this task exposes a tension between a quest for standardization, uniformity, or normalization (FIU 2014) and a respect for the unique attributes of the object and the librarian's stewardship of it. For example, Martha Yee, Cataloging Supervisor, UCLA Film and Television Archive, writes:

> "Can all bibliographic data be reduced to either a class or a property with a finite list of values? Another way to put this is to ask if all that catalogers do could be reduced to a set of pull-down menus. Cataloging is the art of writing discursive prose as much as it is the ability to select the correct value for a particular data element." (Yee 2009), p. 14.

The projects described in this chapter answer Dr. Yee's question with a qualified 'yes.' Though a linked data model promises to automate many of the routine tasks in the cataloging workflow, it does not eliminate the need for discursive prose. Thus the results support the claim that linked data representations are consistent with existing norms, demonstrating a continued need for the social model of cataloging that has been practiced since the 1970s in a more robust architecture. In the linked data paradigm, the essential problem is the assignment of URIs to the resources being described—to objects in hand as well as to more abstract interpretations of creative works—and resolving the URIs to authoritative descriptions about them.

If this problem is not solved, the referents of a bibliographic description will remain lost in an ever-expanding sea of text, and redundant effort will continue to be expended in uncoordinated attempts to describe the same work or edition. But if the problem can be solved, the result will be a set of authoritative references for creative works where none existed before, an outcome that promises to promote standardization in the cataloging workflow and automate some routine tasks. This chapter and the next describe how authoritative hubs for Works and Objects are being built at OCLC. Our solution is derived from a conceptual model of Works developed in the library community and modeled in Schema.org, which we have expanded with a newly defined companion vocabulary called BiblioGraph (BGN 2014a) that extends the referential scope of Schema.org to resources of interest to the library community and the cultural heritage sector.

The references are populated with data mined from WorldCat and VIAF. In Chapter 5, we will comment on the implications of these projects for future descriptive practice.

3.2   THE FRBR GROUP I CONCEPTUAL MODEL

The ontology of creative works is the subject of the seminal report *Functional Requirements for Bibliographic Records* (IFLA-SG 1998), which describes a conceptual model of the contents of a library catalog developed in the 1990s. The FRBR model defines creative works as 'the product of intellectual and artistic endeavor that are named or described in bibliographic records,' and are connected through a chain of relationships to 'Expressions,' 'Manifestations,' and 'Items.' As illustrated in the widely reproduced diagram shown in Figure 3.1, a Work is realized through an Expression, which is embodied in a Manifestation and exemplified by an Item.

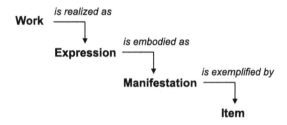

Figure 3.1: The FRBR Group I, or 'Works' hierarchy. Adapted from Tillett (2004).

The best arguments for the FRBR Group I model come from the description of canonical works of world literature, which have been translated, adapted, commented upon, and republished for hundreds of years, but have their source in a single identifiable act of creative endeavor. Shakespeare's *Hamlet* is a good example. As a Work, *Hamlet* is like the name of a law or a theorem or a hymn, whose real-world referent might be conveyed through a definition in a dictionary, library authority file, or Wikipedia page, and whose reality seems independent of any particular tangible realization. As an Expression, *Hamlet* is a unique text, originally written in English and translated, annotated, summarized, performed on stage, or made into a movie. As a Manifestation, the text representing a single Expression of *Hamlet* may be physically realized as a paperback edition published in New York in 1992 by St. Martin's Press. And as an Item, a used copy of the Methuen edition of *Hamlet* can be purchased from Amazon.com or borrowed from the Capital University Library in Columbus, Ohio. The FRBR Group I model is less compelling when applied to more obscure works such as Roger Hilsman's *American Guerrilla*, the World War II memoir we described in Section 1.3 of Chapter 1, because this book has a much shorter publication history and no derivatives have yet been produced. Yet a search on WorldCat.org returns a list of 10 versions that can be interpreted as different Manifestations: a hardback, a paperback, and an e-book available from Hathi Trust that was digitized in 2010 from the hardback edition published by Profile Books in 1990.

The Resource Description and Access specification (RDA 2010) develops the FRBR model into a rich set of vocabularies that define more precise relationships among the levels in the FRBR Works hierarchy and the agents involved in their production. For example, a scan of the appendices in the RDA Toolkit reveals that Works and Expressions are related to one another by relationships such as 'Motion Picture Adaptation of', 'Analysis of', and 'Translation of.' Manifestations are related through relationships such as 'Also issued as' and 'Special Issue of.' Finally, Items are connected through relationships such 'Facsimile of' and 'Reproduction of,' which are useful for describing digitial objects and their physical sources, which we discuss briefly in the final section of this chapter. When these relationships are added to the rich set of roles for creators and contributors defined in the 60 years of library resource description by cataloging rules expressed in the MARC standard, it is clear that what could be said about the web of creative works and the agents that bring them into being far exceeds the descriptive capacity of Schema.org, which recognizes only a small subset of these connections.

OCLC researchers have been full partners in the development and assessment of FRBR and, to a lesser extent, RDA. For example, Hickey, O'Neill, and Toves (2002) describes an algorithm for inducing the FRBR 'Works' hierarchy from a corpus of MARC records such as those contributed to WorldCat, which has been applied in many research projects conducted at OCLC and elsewhere in the library community (Tillett 2003). A year later, OCLC researchers started with Smiralgia (2001) declaration that the Work is an "essential component of the modern catalog" and highlighted the broader significance of FRBR in terms that are still relevant to our current work:

> "FRBR's core insight is that a set of entities can be identified which are key to the successful use of bibliographic records, e.g., a work, a person, or an event. These entities are related to one another in a variety of ways—e.g., a work may be created by a person, or an event may be the subject of a work. Finally, each entity is characterized by a set of attributes. A work, for example, may be defined by a title, creation date, context, etc.; a person may have a name, title, birth and/or death date, etc. This approach emphasizes not individual data elements in the bibliographic record per se, but rather the entities, relationships, and attributes the bibliographic record is intended to describe." (Bennett, Lavoie, and O'Neill 2002)

The Bennett team argued that an entity-relationship model supports expanded options for browsing and searching a library catalog, making it possible to satisfy information requests even when they are fuzzy or vague. But given the reservations about some of the details of the FRBR Group I model—that a Work may be indistinguishable from a text (Genz 2002), that the definitions of Work and Expression overlap (O'Neill 2002; Tillett 2004), and that many resources do not require the 'full FRBR treatment' (IFLA 2014)—a literal formalization such as the one proposed by Hillmann et al. (2002) is unrealistic, for reasons we discuss in more detail below. Instead, the OCLC research program on FRBR supports an argument for a computationally realistic model that approximates the FRBR definitions and gathers evidence for the Group I entities by mining a large corpus of bibliographic descriptions. The research cited here hints at these conclusions, but the linked data model described in the next section of this chapter makes them more explicit.

The most visible outcome of the early research projects conducted at OCLC was the re-design of WorldCat.org as a hierarchical display. For important works such as Charles Darwin's *On the Origin of Species*, such an organization is especially urgent because users would otherwise be confronted with list of search results spanning multiple pages. But in the hierarchical display, now visible in WorldCat.org, the reader first encounters a description of the FRBR Work. From there, the reader can click on the 'View all editions and formats' link to view the expanded list of pointers that link to over a thousand hardback, paperback, digitized, and microform versions of the book. The resources described at these links can be interpreted as FRBR Manifestations.

In addition to the results viewable in WorldCat.org, research investigations of the FRBR Group I model have produced utilities, services, and demonstration projects that connect library resources to the wider community of information seekers. For example, the 'xISBN Bookmarklet' (OCLC 1998) is a Web-browser plug-in that enables a reader to discover a book of interest on a bookseller website and obtain a copy from a local library with the same or a related ISBN. The 'Metadata Services for Publishers' project (Godby 2010) is part of an OCLC production stream that upgrades publisher-supplied bibliographic records with subject headings, classification num-bers, and authority-controlled names by assigning sparse records to a Work cluster and applying data from richer records found in the same cluster. A project with similar goals is the experimen-tal 'Classify' service (Vizine-Goetz 2014a), which recommends subject headings and classification numbers for a user-submitted title by locating it in a Work cluster and applying subject metadata that has already been assigned.

Mature prototypes demonstrating cleaner, simpler displays of outputs from the FRBR al-gorithms are being developed for future versions of WorldCat.org. For example, in the 'Cookbook Finder' demo (Vizine-Goetz 2013), properties that characterize the Work independently of its physical realization, such as the title, author, summary and other descriptions of the content, are shown at the top of the page, while descriptions of the corresponding Manifestations are available in the section labeled 'Editions' at the bottom of the page. Links to related works, as identified by authority-controlled subject headings, are also prominently displayed. The 'Kindred Works' demo (Vizine-Goetz 2014b) is a companion project that recommends works of similar content identifiable from Work-level descriptions.

Underlying all of these projects are the FRBR data-mining algorithms themselves, which have undergone continuous improvement. In the 16 years since the publication of the first reports, WorldCat has grown from 48 million to over 300 million records, and the algorithms have become both simpler and more robust. We will describe the latest version of the algorithms in more detail in Section 3.5, where we show that they are an integral step in the discovery of evidence for the model of creative works published as the RDF statements accessible from WorldCat.org.

3.3   FRBR IN THE WEB OF DATA

OCLC's research supports the conclusion that at least two levels must be recognized in the FRBR Group I hierarchy. A creative work is an abstract idea that prompts the user's information request, which corresponds roughly to a FRBR Work. A creative work is also the physical or tangible object that ultimately satisfies the request, which can be modeled as a FRBR Manifestation or Item.

As we have seen, OCLC's implementation of this distinction is designed to facilitate searching and simplify the display of WorldCat.org and individual library catalogs. But it is now becoming visible in the Web beyond the library community. For example, Figure 3.2 shows the English-language Wikipedia page for *On the Origin of Species*. The Infobox on the right side of the page is reproduced in the magnified inset in the center of the image. It is populated with authoritative structured data, including the publication date, a digital image of the title page of the first edition, and a link to the same work in described WorldCat.org. A Google search for *Origin of Species* produces a front page with the Knowledge Card shown on the right, which cites Wikipedia as a source and contains some of the same structured data.

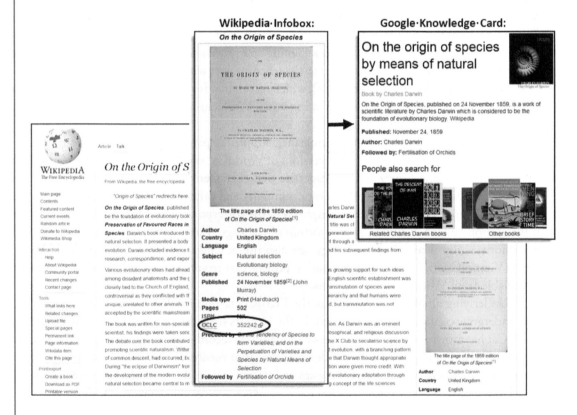

Figure 3.2: Works as structured data in Wikipedia and Google.

These examples demonstrate the theoretical possibility that library resource descriptions could be exposed to the wider Web, where a reader could search for a creative work on Google or Wikipedia and follow a link to a nearby library to obtain an object with the desired physical characteristics. But today this vision is only partly realized. The link to WorldCat.org resolves to a page that is still too difficult to navigate. And the Google Knowledge Card contains a link only to the HarperCollins edition published in 2012, but not to any of the other editions and formats described in WorldCat—including the original edition, which is highlighted on the Wikipedia page. Such gaps and inconsistencies imply a need for a more abstract conception of the Work such as the one we have discussed, which libraries and aggregators of library metadata such as OCLC are in the best position to define. When it matures, a model of the creative work that includes this level of description would rectify a larger problem than any of the shortcomings pointed out here. Neither Wikipedia Infoboxes nor Google Knowledge Cards even exist for the vast majority of resources held by libraries because they are not exposed as structured data on the Web at all.

To address these problems, we are packaging the library community's understanding of creative works 'in the form that the Web wants,' to use a phrase popularized by our OCLC colleague Richard Wallis (Wallis 2014b). In operational terms, this means that the output of OCLC's FRBR data-mining algorithms are being integrated into the model of creative works derived from Schema.org that underlies the linked data markup published on catalog records accessible from WorldCat.org. An account of how this is done occupies the rest of this chapter.

3.4   THE OCLC MODEL OF WORKS

OCLC's model of creative works is grounded in the conviction that the fundamental interactions between information seekers and creative works that motivated the FRBR Group I conceptual model—finding, identifying, selecting, and obtaining—are as relevant on the wider Web as they are in a single library catalog and must be represented in a formal model. But as we have seen, it is difficult to design a model of Works, Expressions, Manifestations and Items that is applicable across the broad spectrum of resource types managed by libraries and to discover evidence for these distinctions in legacy bibliographic descriptions. The problem arises because the four concepts defined in the Group I hierarchy are typically modeled as classes, making it necessary to define rules that can distinguish them. We are exploring the alternative hypothesis that much of the FRBR Group I model is expressible through properties defined on just two classes—namely, schema:CreativeWork and schema:Product, which can be used to define a set of connections among Works, People, Objects, Organizations, Places, and Concepts involved in the creation, production, and management of intellectual capital by libraries and other communities with similar interests. The result is a lightweight, flexible model that can be discovered by mining WorldCat or other collections of bibliographic records.

Figure 3.3 shows a high-level web of relationships for all six of the key entities we have discussed throughout this book, this time in more technical detail. In fact, the figure is simply a variant of Figure 1.1, the very first figure displayed in Chapter 1. At the center is the distinction

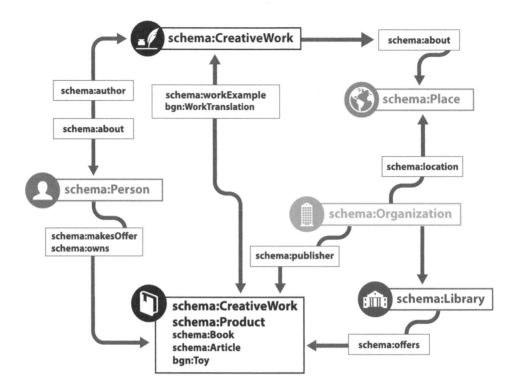

Figure 3.3: The top-level view of the OCLC model of Works.

between the Work as content and the Work as a product or object, enhanced with a set of relationships that can be derived from research on FRBR and RDA. Thus, a Work can be a translation of another Work, such as a German translation of *Beowulf*; a Work can originate from the same act of creative endeavor as another Work, as when *Hamlet* is realized either as a play or as a book for young adults; or a Work can be viewed as a Product, which is borrowed from a library or lent to a patron. A Work can also be 'about' a Person, Place, or Organization. The other key entities also have relationships with creative works, such as the Person acting as an author who creates content; the Organization acting as a publisher that transforms the content into a product; or a library, a subclass of Organization, which acquires, lends, and licenses the product to patrons. Though the model is a variant of a hub-and-spoke design with two types of creative works in the center, the key entities may also have relationships with one another, such as the 'location' relationship between an Organization and a Place that could be defined in a lower level of modeling detail.

Schema.org provides a rich foundation for the definition of creative works that can support the needs of libraries, but the labels shown in Figure 3.3 identify an additional source of vocabulary. As expected, terms defined in the 'schema:' namespace represent concepts imported from

Schema.org for naming the most important classes and subclasses and many properties. In addition, terms defined in the 'bgn:' namespace represent concepts imported from BiblioGraph.net, an experimental extension vocabulary for Schema.org developed by OCLC researchers for the description of library resources in a format suitable for use by the information-seeking public on the wider Web (BGN 2014a). BiblioGraph.net is a more sophisticated implementation of the experimental 'library' vocabulary published in the first- generation RDF markup on World-Cat.org and has been heavily influenced by the principles and recommendations of the W3C-sponsored Schema Bib Extend Community Group (Schema Bib Extend 2014d), about which we have more to say below. In building out the model, our goal is to define additional subclasses of schema:CreativeWork and properties that define a more detailed view of library resources, from which a high-level model of typical library transactions such as acquiring, lending, and preserving can eventually be defined. Taken together, these concepts and their interrelationships comprise OCLC's model of creative works—or simply 'Works,' to use the term we have mentioned throughout this book.

3.4.1 EXTENDING SCHEMA.ORG

In Schema.org, CreativeWork is a subclass of schema:Thing, for which properties such as 'name' and 'description' have been defined. Properties for schema:CreativeWork include those typically mentioned in the descriptions of FRBR Works and Manifestations, such as schema:publisher, schema:datePublished, schema:typicalAgeRange, schema:inLanguage, schema:about, and so on. Subclasses of CreativeWork defined by Schema.org include schema:Book, which supplies a set of even more specific properties such as schema:numberOfPages and schema:illustrator. Thus the class and property chains in Schema.org ontology are both hierarchically structured and flexible, which we exploit in the design of the OCLC model of Works. Refinements to Schema.org can be made with relative ease because of relaxed requirements for type assignments. Though the hierarchy labeled with the terms 'Thing - CreativeWork - Book' defines a class and property chain, all of the properties are optional and may even move up the chain—forming, in effect, a loosely typed universe of descriptors from which a set of more or less detailed statements about a resource can be constructed.

The draft specification for the enhanced vocabulary available from BiblioGraph.net has the same organization as Schema.org because it is derived from the same open source software platform. Built from Python scripts and cascading style sheets, the software creates displayable pages from a source file containing the complete vocabulary specification for Schema.org represented in the RDFa Lite format (Schema 2012). The OCLC project team has added a corresponding RDFa Lite file containing the BiblioGraph extensions (BGN 2014b), modified the stylesheets to produce some lightweight BiblioGraph branding, and enhanced the software to accept multiple namespaces and type inheritances. To keep the two vocabularies synchronized, the process for building BiblioGraph.net uses the latest copy of the Schema.org and merges it with the Biblio-

Graph extensions. Duplicate terms are managed in these specification files, which identifies the presence of the 'supersedes' and 'supersededBy' relationships between terms.

For example, the class bgn:Agent, defined as a parent of schema:Person and schema:Organization, contains two new properties, bgn:publishedBy and bgn:translator. This class permits accurate statements about creative works when the class membership of the creator, translator, or publisher is unspecified or irrelevant. Most BiblioGraph terms define new properties or subclasses of schema:CreativeWork, such as bgn:Newspaper, bgn:Thesis, bgn:Chapter, or bgn:MusicScore. Since most extensions are straighforward, it is easy to imagine how they would be positioned in the Schema.org ontology. But other subclasses are ontologically more complex. For example, bgn:Toy takes advantage of multiple type inheritance, an under-documented feature of Schema.org that is a consequence of its compatibility with RDF-Schema (Brickley 2010; Ronallo 2013). With two parents, a toy can be interpreted from two points of view. As a subclass of schema:CreativeWork, it can be understood as a genre or resource type analogous to schema:Book or schema:Movie. But described as a schema:Product, a toy can also be understood as a real-world object that can be bought, sold, lent, borrowed, and played with.

Multiple inheritance from the schema:CreativeWork and schema:Product class hierarchies is instrumental in drawing the distinction between the Work as Content and the Work as Object that is fundamental to the OCLC model of Works. As shown in Figure 3.4, subclasses of schema:Product introduce concepts that make it possible to refer to creative works realized as unique objects or as identical members of a set. Thus schema:IndividualProduct is "a single, identifiable product instance (e.g., a laptop with a particular serial number)" (Schema.org 2014b) and schema:ProductModel is a "model or vendor specification for a product" (Schema.org 2014a), while schema:SomeProducts is a subset of identical objects that are not individually identifiable.

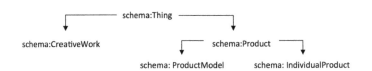

Figure 3.4: Creative Works and the 'Product' hierarchy in Schema.org.

With properties available both from schema:CreativeWork and schema:Product, different kinds of assertions can be expressed about the 'Toy' class defined in BiblioGraph.net, which might be associated with lifecycle events. For example, a set of statements that make the dual rdf:type assignments of schema:CreativeWork and schema:IndividualProduct can describe a unique creation by the creator, who may have designed a prototype electronic game that teaches children to write by tracing lights on a small console with a stylus. Once the game is manufactured and made available for sale from Amazon.com, it is assigned the product identifier 'B001W2WKS0', which uniquely identifies the version of *LeapFrog Scribble and Write* produced by LeapFrog in 2014. Since a product identifier can be interpreted as a model number, the set of objects with the same code can be described as a schema:ProductModel. When this version of the game is purchased, a single exemplar is sent to the buyer–which, like the original prototype, is described as schema:IndividualProduct and schema:CreativeWork. But now it is a member of a set of identical manufactured objects, a reality that be expressed linked through a statement containing the property schema:model, which associates the object with a description of the corresponding schema:ProductModel class. When the physical realization is not known or does not matter, however, as in the assignment of intellectual property rights, no value from the Schema:Product class needs to be assigned at all and the single type assignment schema:CreativeWork is sufficient.

3.4.2   MODELING FRBR CONCEPTS IN SCHEMA.ORG AND BIBLIOGRAPH

The flexible design features of Schema.org and the BiblioGraph extension vocabulary are used to build out a model of Works that recognizes the most important distinctions captured in the FRBR Group I model. At the highest level, the model establishes a one-to-many relationship between an abstract creative work and a set of creative-work 'objects' and expresses it through reciprocal links accessible from WorldCat.org and WorldCat Works (OCLC 2014b), an RDF dataset that defines clusters of library resources described in WorldCat catalog data that have the same content-oriented properties. Though designed for machine consumption, a World-Cat Work description can be viewed through the human-readable 'WorldCat Linked Data Explorer' interface when a known URI is supplied. Some examples are discussed below. As shown schematically in Figure 3.5, this model asserts an abstract, or null, relationship between resources typed as schema:CreativeWork, defined using the generic properties schema:workExample and schema:exampleOfWork. These terms were proposed as extensions by the Schema Bib Extend Community Group in early 2014 and have recently been been adopted by Schema.org (Wallis 2014a).

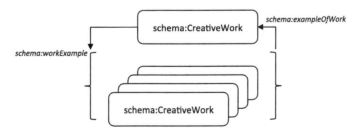

Figure 3.5: A Work and a set of Work Examples.

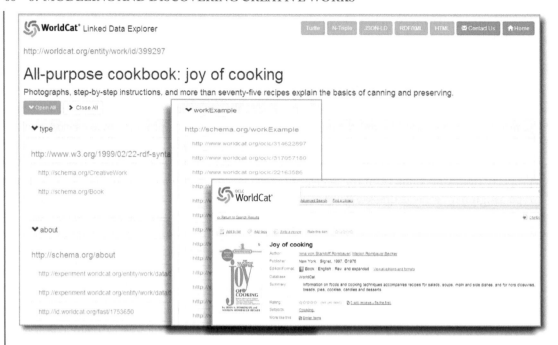

Figure 3.6: A link from WorldCat.org to WorldCat Works.

The same relationships are shown in more concrete detail through evidence discoverable from a search on WorldCat.org for the edition of *Joy of Cooking* published by Scribner in 1997. Figure 3.6 shows the two types of resources. In the foreground, in the bottom right corner of the image, is a page accessible from a WorldCat search describing a human-readable summary of a MARC record. It is recast in this model as a 'Work example,' defined in Schema.org as an "...Example/instance/realization/derivation of the concept of this creative work" (Schema.org 2014c). In the background is the corresponding 'Work' page defined in WorldCat Works, which contains RDF statements describing the title, author, subject headings, summaries, and other content-oriented metadata applicable to all versions of *Joy of Cooking* when viewed from a higher level of abstraction that omits the details of physical realization. The image in the center is an excerpt from the list of schema:workExample statements available from the WorldCat Works page, which identifies the complete set of URIs for the corresponding resources described in WorldCat to which the 'Work' description applies.

Excerpts from the corresponding RDF/Turtle instance data are shown in Figure 3.7. In the first block, the WorldCat 'Work' is typed as schema:CreativeWork and contains proper-ties defined by Schema.org for the content-oriented metadata. This block is linked by a set of schema:workExample statements to a collection of published editions, one of which is referenced in the second group of statements. These statements have been selected from the description pub-

```
<http://worldcat.org/entity/work/id/399297>
a schema:CreativeWork;
    schema:name "Joy of Cooking";
    schema:author "Rombauer, Irma von Starkloff, 1877-1962";
    schema:about <http://id.worldcat.org/fast/1753224>;
    schema:about "Cooking, American";
    schema:description "Since its original publication, Joy of Cooking has been the most
authoritative cookbook in America - the one upon which millions of cooks have confidently
relied for more than sixty-five years."
    schema:workExample <http://www.worldcat.org/37801353>.


<http://worldcat.org/37801353>
a schema:CreativeWork, schema:ProductModel;
    schema:name "Joy of Cooking";
    schema:author "Rombauer, Irma von Starkloff, 1877-1962";
    schema:publisher "Scribners";
    schema:dateOfPublication "1997";
    schema:isbn "0684818701";
    schema:about <http://id.worldcat.org/fast/1753224>;
    schema:about "Cooking, American".
    schema:exampleOfWork <http://worldcat.org/entity/work/id/399297>.
```

Figure 3.7: RDF/Turtle instance data for two kinds of Works.

lished in the 'Linked Data' section of the WorldCat.org page for the 1997 Scribners edition shown in Figure 3.6. The statements in this block also refer to an object typed as schema:CreativeWork. But because this description contains details that identify the referent as a particular class of products manufactured in the publisher supply chain, such as a publisher, publication date, page count, and ISBN, a data-mining process applied to WorldCat can discover evidence that justifies an additional type assignment of schema:ProductModel. Because of the difference in RDF type assignments, a machine process can distinguish between the two kinds of creative work.

Thus the relationship between a Work and a 'Work example' is akin to the relationship between a FRBR Work and a Manifestation. If the object is a printed book or a manufactured CD that is a member of a set of identical exemplars, the description will typically contain product identifiers such as ISBNs. If it is an e-journal or e-book, the description will contain properties that identify ISSNs or DOIs. Though many characteristics of creative works produced by commercial publishers can already be described by properties defined in Schema.org, extensions defined in the BiblioGraph extension vocabulary will be required to describe those of special interest to libraries, such as unique manuscripts, archives, theses or digitized collections. But from the perspective of

```
<http://ghpl.org/0684818701/12345>
schema:CreativeWork, schema:IndividualProduct;
    schema:name "Joy of Cooking";
    schema:author "Rombauer, Irma von Starkloff, 1877-1962";
    schema:dateOfPublication "1997";
    schema:isbn "0684818701";
    schema:description "641.5 ROM";
    schema:model <http://www.worldcat.org/37801353>.
```

Figure 3.8: A hypothetical RDF/Turtle description of a library's copy of *Joy of Cooking*.

the larger Schema.org ontology, all physical or tangible objects justify a type assignment from the schema:Product, which makes Works as Objects ontologically distinct from Works as Content without triggering the need to recognize a separate class such as 'frbr:Manifestation' in the model.

This model is easily extended to include a FRBR-inspired Item. Figure 3.8 shows a hypothetical set of RDF statements describing a copy of the Scribners edition of *Joy of Cooking* available from Grandview Heights Public Library. Like the companion description of the Manifestation shown in Figure 3.7, the RDF representation identifies an author, title, and publication details. But because this description refers to a copy, it contains additional properties that trigger the assignment of schema:IndividualProduct, such as a unique shelf location, captured here in the schema:description field; or, more plausibly, a barcode or spine label. The relationship between the Manifestation and Item can be captured by the property schema:model, already defined for schema:Product, which can be fashioned into a statement about set membership. This copy of *Joy of Cooking* is identified as an exemplar of the product whose description is accessible from World-Cat.org at the URI ending in 37801353.

The hypothetical copy of *Joy of Cooking* available from Grandview Heights Public Library presents an opportunity to point out two design features of OCLC model of Works: a more flexible model of FRBR Group I concepts, and a richer and ontologically more natural model of holdings than the existing record-oriented descriptive practice. In current systems, a library holding is a noun, or a 'Thing,' perhaps because a status bit is set in an aggregated database of bibliographic records such as WorldCat whenever a library claims ownership of a particular title. But outside the context of a record-oriented architecture, a library holding is expressed more intuitively as a relationship involving a library, a creative work, and terms of access. A high-level view of a model that is consistent with the OCLC model of Works is shown in Figure 3.9.

The multicolored ribbons in the diagram illustrate the FRBR-like distinctions between Work, Manifestation, and Item implicit in the RDF statements shown in Figures 3.7 and 3.8. A set of statements about a volume with a complex publication history such as *Joy of Cooking* makes reference to these three concepts, but the diagram implies that links to Work and Manifestation descriptions may not be necessary for some kinds of resources. For example, if the Item in the col-

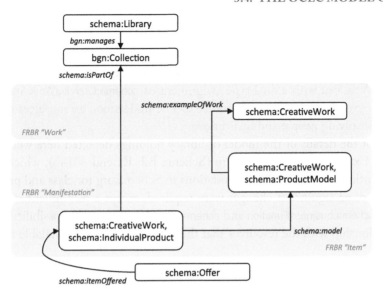

Figure 3.9: A library holding expressed as a schema:Offer.

lection is a unique object, such as a handwritten journal or a collection of photographs assembled by a local historical society, the resource could be described as a schema:IndividualProduct, which would not require a schema:model link to other concepts defined in the FRBR Group I hierarchy.

To account for library holdings, the model is extended in two ways. First, the model must describe the larger context of a library with at least one collection. A library can be identified with schema:Library, but a suitable concept of 'Collection' may require a refinement of the existing Schema.org draft or a redefinition as a term of art in the BiblioGraph namespace. A hypothetical property such as bgn:manage could associate the library with its collection; and once connected, the schema:isPartOf property can identify the held item as a member of the collection. But the most novel part of this analysis stems from the description of the library's terms of accessibility in the schema:Offer class. For example, a rich set of schema:Offer properties such as schema:businessFunction, schema:itemAvailability, schema:availabilityStarts and schema:availabilityEnds can be used to craft a detailed description specifying that a book can be lent for a two-week period to library cardholders, who are levied a fine if it is returned after the due date, and so on. The schema:Offer class is linked to the schema:Product hierarchy by the schema:itemOffered property, creating a point of entry into the GoodRelations ontology (Hepp 2014), which was recently absorbed into Schema.org.

Though designed for commerce, the properties and classes defined in GoodRelations make it possible to publish the business logic of an important library transaction in a format that is completely machine-processable and capable of interpretation by general-purpose search engines. Current library catalogs derive their implementations from the MARC 21 Format for Holdings standard (LC 2000) to define a locally maintained record consisting primarily of human-readable text that lists the title, author, and product and item identifiers, and describes the unique physical location of the item on a particular shelf in a building. Such records are difficult to maintain and are accessible only from the software applications maintained by the library and are not visible on the broader Web. But with a dual type assignment of schema:CreativeWork and a value from the schema:Product vocabulary, a library resource can be understood as an object that participates in transactions involving people and institutions.

Most of the details of the model of library holdings depicted here were developed in the Schema Bib Extend Community Group (Schema Bib Extend 2014b), which took on the task with the intention of making recommendations to Schema.org for class and property extensions. But in the end, no significant changes were required, except a recommendation to broaden the meaning of schema:businessFunction and schema:seller to include the possibility that libraries have a 'vend' relationship with the resources that they manage and make available to patrons.

Modeling FRBR Expressions

The discussion above has shown that the OCLC model of Works accounts for the differences between Work as Content and Work as Object by making reference to the properties listed in a resource description, many of which have already been defined in Schema.org. Though some differences in detail are ontologically significant, resources typed as schema:CreativeWork have been linked with one another only by the semantically non-committal properties schema:workExample and schema:exampleOfWork.

What is missing in the model is an account of Content-to-Content relationships, which are interpreted in the FRBR Group I model as relationships between Works and Expressions. As described in the FRBR and RDA scholarship, Expressions of the same Work produce different texts or performances—as a translation, a revision, an adaptation, a new edition, a new arrangement, or other changes that largely preserve the creative intent of the original endeavor. But as we noted in the previous section, even the earliest research on FRBR revealed fuzzy boundaries between FRBR Works and Expressions. Recent studies have renewed the argument that an ontologically distinct FRBR Expression is valuable for use cases that identify commonalities among some creative works (Zumer, O'Neill, and Mixter 2015), but the complexity introduced by an additional concept must be weighed against the problem of requiring distinctions that may be difficult to discover algorithmically.

In the context of the OCLC model of Works, this uncertainty implies that the evidence discoverable in bibliographic descriptions is insufficient to justify the definition of a class in the model such as 'frbr:Expression.' Instead, the Content-to-Content relationships that underlie the reality of FRBR-like Expressions are expressed as properties of schema:CreativeWork. Accumulating evidence discovered by a data mining algorithm operating on bibliographic metadata can trigger a more specific property than schema:workExample, such as 'is translation of,' 'is adapta-

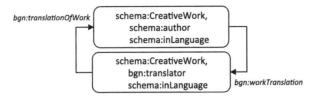

Figure 3.10: Translation relationships between a Work and a Manifestation.

tion of,' or any number of other relationships that have already been proposed. We illustrate this feature of the model using OCLC's Multilingual WorldCat project.

Nearly half of the bibliographic descriptions in WorldCat are written in languages other than English, many representing translations of humanity's most important cultural and intellectual heritage (Smith-Yoshimura 2014b; Gatenby 2013). The records in this subset of WorldCat consist primarily of textual descriptions that are not machine-understandable. But at its core, an improved model of translations must recognize three properties: the language of the target text, the language of the source text, and the 'translation' relationship between the source and the target. A more complete description would also include the name of the translator and properties that encode the text, such as character sets, character encodings, and transliteration schemes. The schematic in Figure 3.10 suggests that all characteristics except the 'translation' relationship can be defined as properties on schema:CreativeWork. Some, such as schema:inLanguage, are already part of the standard; others, such as bgn:translator, are being defined in the BiblioGraph.net extension vocabulary. But since translations are Content-to-Content relationships among resources typed as schema:CreativeWork, they are linked by the more specific properties bgn:workTranslation and bgn:translationOfWork instead of the generic schema:workExample and schema:exampleOfWork.

Figure 3.11 illustrates a network of relationships that can be induced from data available from WorldCat for a Chinese-language Work translated into English as *Journey to the West*. Details about the source description are shown in the orange box and the corresponding details for English, Vietnamese, German, and Japanese translations are shown in green boxes. The color coding is consistent with the with the model of holdings shown in Figure 3.9 and implies a Work-Manifestation relationship between the 16th-century Chinese novel and its derivatives. This example has been simplified for ease of exposition, but WorldCat catalog records contain an abundance of detail that would trigger a type assignment from the schema:Product class on the derivatives—such as publication dates, publishers, and page counts—which is absent in the description of the source. In effect, the figure implies that Content-to-Content relationships such as 'translation of Work' and the properties important for drawing distinctions in the FRBR Group I hierarchy in the OCLC model of Works are orthogonal and can freely co-occur.

As in the model of library holdings, the research on multilingual bibliographic descriptions underscores an important difference between the OCLC model of Works and previous implementations of the FRBR Group I conceptual model: the hierarchical relationship among Work,

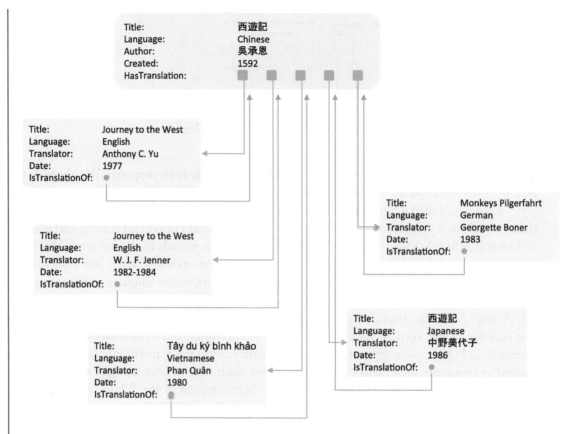

Figure 3.11: A classic Chinese novel and some translations. Adapted from Smith-Yoshimura (2014b).

Expression, Manifestation, and Item is not required or even presupposed. It is simply one possible configuration among many.

For example, Figure 3.12 shows relationships among translations of Hans Christian Andersen's fairy tale *Snedronningen* in slightly more detail. At the bottom of the figure is a MARC description for an English translation of *Snow Queen*, which contains publication details that generate a schema:ProductModel type assignment and can be interpreted as a Manifestation. The MARC description reveals that the source is a German translation titled *Schneekönigin*, not the Danish original. According to a note in the MARC description, the German translation was first published in Switzerland, but it does not contain enough evidence to identify a particular edition. Since WorldCat contains many German translations of *Snedronningen*, a Work cluster can be inferred. A Work cluster of English translations can also be inferred, which contains the version of *Snow Queen* translated by Anthea Bell as a member, or a 'Work example.' But inside the cluster of

English translations, the translation sources may differ; what is known for certain is only that the source for the Bell translation is an unspecified member of the German translation Work cluster. This relationship is captured with bgn:workTranslation and bgn:translationOfWork properties between the English Manifestation and the German Work shown in the diagram.

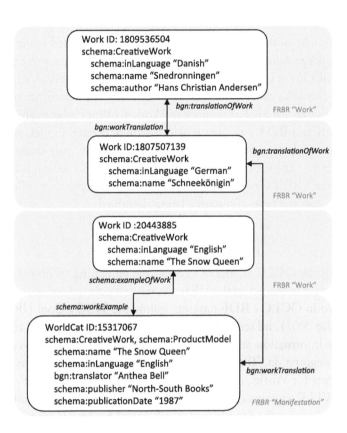

Figure 3.12: A Manifestation with multiple translation sources.

In effect, the Multilingual WorldCat project provides much-needed empirical input to a model of translations. Instead of encoding a theoretical pronouncement that a translation is a relationship between Works, or between a Work and an Expression, a model derived from data can describe a more nuanced reality. Sometimes the translation source is a chain of translations that lead only indirectly to the original work, as Figure 3.12 shows. Sometimes the translation is derived from a particular Manifestation and has sibling relationships to other translations, but often the textual source of the translation is not specified at all.

Summary: FRBR in the OCLC Model of Works

As we first pointed out in the discussion of Figure 3.1, previous formalizations had translated the FRBR Group I model, and the RDA elaborations of it, into a class hierarchy with exactly four levels, connected by properties with rigidly specified domains and ranges. For example, the RDA Relationship ontologies define 'Translation of' as a relationship between Expressions, while 'Contained in' is a relationship between Manifestations (RDA 2010). But in the OCLC model of Works, the hierarchy of the FRBR data model has been flattened while retaining the essential meaning of the concept definitions. This result is accomplished by representing three of the categories in the FRBR Group I Model as instances of schema:CreativeWork with different properties, assigning a value from the schema:Product ontology if certain details are present, and redefining the relationships among FRBR Expressions as Work-to-Work relationships. Thus the hierarchical model of FRBR and RDA has been replaced with a 'trigger' model, which means that most schema:CreativeWork properties are not ontologically distinctive; only those that imply physicality or set membership are. The most important consequence of this design is that the concepts originally defined in the FRBR Group I hierarchy can expand, repeat, or collapse depending on the quality of the data and the type of resource being described.

3.4.3   A NOTE ABOUT URI DESIGN

In this overview of the OCLC model of Works, one remaining technical detail needs to be discussed: the syntax and semantics of the URIs. As we first pointed out in Section 1.3 of Chapter 1, all URIs published in OCLC's RDF datasets follow the W3C's Cool URIs convention (Sauermann and Cyganiac 2007) and resolve via the HTTP 303 direct protocol to a Generic Document with authoritative information about the resource, whose format is delivered to the users device through content negotiation. The pages available from WorldCat Works can be understood as Generic Documents for Works, as can some pages available from VIAF. The end of Chapter 2 pointed out that VIAF contains descriptions of more than two million uniform titles, an artifact of the traditional library authority file that is still useful because it contains highly reliable, controlled strings representing the original title of a Work and its translated forms recognized by the library community. *Joy of Cooking* is among the many Works that do not have a uniform title description, but a VIAF description accessible at http://viaf.org/viaf/185090227 is available for the Chinese literary classic translated as *Journey to the West*, which is depicted in Figure 3.11. The Cool URIs convention permits RDF statements asserting that the VIAF URI and the URI associated with the corresponding WorldCat Works page refer to the same real-world object.

The syntax of the URIs is still in flux because several experiments are being conducted in parallel and must be compatible with legacy data stores and software processes. As the instance data excerpted in Figure 3.8 shows, the special status of a WorldCat Works URI as an identifier for a Work entity can be parsed from the token sequence http://worldcat.org/entity/work/id. But it is associated by the schema:exampleOfWork property with legacy WorldCat URLs, such as http://www.worldcat.org/37801353, from which no such interpretation can be inferred.

Right now, the referent of the WorldCat URL is a bibliographic record, but it is expected to evolve into a schema:CreativeWork realized as a FRBR Manifestation when the model of creative works described in WorldCat is more mature. The URI could be expected to have the form worldcat.org/entity/manifestation/id, matching the pattern of the WorldCat Works URI, but such a design is not required for fully RDF-aware software processes that can read the description directly to identify the referent as a schema:CreativeWork. Once RDF datasets and software environments achieve critical mass, we may opt to redesign the URIs as semantically opaque strings analogous to those now available from VIAF.

3.4.4 BIBLIOGRAPH: A CURATED VOCABULARY FOR SCHEMA.ORG

OCLC's model of Works is derived from Schema.org and supplemented with vocabulary defined in BiblioGraph, which uses linked data principles and practices to describe entities and relationships that matter to those interested in the domain of bibliographic description. To echo the language used by R.V. Guha and other Semantic Web experts, this design responds to those who have both simple and complex things to say about resources that need to be more easily discoverable on the Web. Thus Schema.org was designed as an easy-to-use vocabulary for webmasters, which purposely omits the specialized vocabularies of individual professions or communities of practice. But linked data models in all domains are still immature and evolving rapidly, and even general-purpose vocabularies such as Schema.org still have genuine gaps.

As we said above, BiblioGraph is a proving ground for supplementing Schema.org with vocabulary required for the development of models in the domain of library resource management. BiblioGraph addresses two long-term goals. The first is to identify simple, commonsense terms such as 'translation,' which are intuitively comprehensible and potentially useful to the information-seeking public. The second goal is to identify terms such as 'Agent' that permit true but complex statements about our domain that may be of interest only to professional managers of bibliographic description. The distinction may be subtle, but it is clearly drawn in the model. The first term is a candidate for formal inclusion in the Schema.org vocabulary and would be represented as schema:translation. The second term retains its definition in the BiblioGraph namespace as bgn:Agent, though it can be positioned in the formal structure of the Schema.org vocabulary. A team of editors and advisers will conduct the analysis required to accomplish these goals as they continue to develop the BiblioGraph vocabulary.

In the process of defining the domain of bibliographic description, the BiblioGraph editors have also discovered accidental gaps in Schema.org. For example, 'Toy' is clearly not a technical term unique to librarianship, though a MARC record accessible from WorldCat.org reveals that the electronic game *Twist & Shout Multiplication*, mentioned earlier, is held by a school library in Noblesville, Indiana. Thus it seems likely that 'Toy' will by added to Schema.org through some pathway not involving BiblioGraph. If this happens, BiblioGraph will be modified to remove the redundant term, as it was when the bgn:VideoGame class was recently deprecated after the same concept was defined in Schema.org.

BiblioGraph has been influenced by OCLC's participation in the W3C Schema Bib Extend Community Group (Schema Bib Extend 2014d), which was convened in 2012 to help Schema.org meet at least the minimal needs of communities with a professional interest in bibliographic description. Among the active participants are authors of the *Library Linked Data Incubator Group Final Report* (Baker et al. 2011), data architects for individual libraries and library service providers, and members of publisher metadata community. Though they represent different constituencies, the members of the Schema Bib Extend Community Group pursue the common goal of monitoring Schema.org for conflicts and redundancies with the most common standards for bibliographic description and making formal recommendations for extensions. In addition, the Schema Bib Extend group lobbies for the use of Schema.org by libraries and works to accelerate its rate of adoption by publishing code samples, recipes, and tutorials (Schema Bib Extend 2014c; Scott 2014).

These successes are possible only through direct engagement with representatives from Schema.org, who ensure that the changes recommended by the library community fall within parameters that minimize the potential for disruption by other data producers. For example, Dan Brickley, who co-chairs the Schema.org task force for extension proposals with R.V. Guha (Guha and Brickley 2014), has specified that only 'non-breaking' changes can be accepted, such as new subclasses, new properties for existing classes, or properties that are promoted to a higher position in a class hierarchy to make them more broadly available. The Schema.org vocabulary also reflects some minor editing changes recommended by the user community. For example, deprecated property names such as CreativeWork-awards were changed from the plural to the singular form CreativeWork-award. BiblioGraph is also modified to remove clashes or redundancies as Schema.org evolves. For example, the bgn:VideoGame class was recently deprecated after the same concept was defined in Schema.org.

Schema.org managers are now formalizing a generic model for extension vocabularies. According to Guha (2015), Bibliograph.net represents a 'reviewed extension,' which is created with a set of contact points with Schema.org, i.e., the new subclasses and properties for existing Schema definitions we have already described. The extension is maintained by editors with backing from a particular community of practice, such as the Schema Bib Extend group. In the proposed new model, the BiblioGraph vocabulary would be uploaded to a Github repository owned by Schema.org, where it could be viewed from an interface accessible from http://bib.schema.org, which would integrate the extension vocabulary with the latest version of Schema.org, much as the Bibliograph.net site does now. Once the extension model is fully implemented, community groups would maintain only their vocabularies, and not the website that delivers it.

3.4.5   OTHER MODELS OF CREATIVE WORKS

OCLC's model of creative works is only one outcome of the redoubled effort focused on bibliographic description undertaken by library standards experts after the publication of the *Library*

Linked Data Incubators Group Report in 2011. Despite the current appearance of the markup, the OCLC model is a direct descendant of the British Library Data Model (Hodson et al. 2012; BL 2014), which predated the publication of Schema.org by several months and was the first large-scale demonstration of a linked data model of bibliographic description by a national library. The most impressive result was that nearly all of the textual fields in a reasonably complex MARC record were represented as URIs, except for irreducible string literals such as titles, summaries, dates, and assorted numerical values.

The British Library Data Model also contains references to many of the same entities recognized in the OCLC model of Works and has a similar configuration. But the British Library model is technically more complex and ontologically more opaque because it is assembled from terms defined in 14 namespaces. A description of *American Guerrilla* is an instructive example because the dataset that accompanies the British Library Data Model has complete RDF/XML and Turtle descriptions of this book and can be directly compared with a description available from WorldCat.org. Table 3.1 shows a simplified description in which the URIs are replaced with text strings corresponding to the name or label of the resource.

Table 3.1: RDF/Turtle instance data from the British Library and OCLC data models

a bibo:BibliographicResource;	a schema:Book;
rdfs:label "American guerrilla";	schema:name "American guerrilla";
dcterms:creator "Roger Hilsman";	schema:author "Roger Hilsman";
blterms:datePublished "2005";	schema:datePublished "2005";
blterms:publication "Potomac";	schema:publisher "Potomac";
dcterms:language "English";	schema:language "English";
dcterms:isPartOf "Memories of War";	schema:collection "Memories of War";
dcterms:subject "Hilsman, Roger";	schema:about "Hilsman, Roger";
dcterms:subject "940.548673092";	schema:about "940.548673092";
bibo:isbn10 "1574886916";	schema:isbn "1574886916";
isbd:01953 "312 p.";	schema:numberOfPages "312 p.";
dcterms:description "includes index"	schema:description "includes index";
dcterms:spatial "Burma"	schema:about "Burma";

The descriptions excerpted in Table 3.1 are equivalent because nearly all of the classes and properties defined in the British Library Data Model can be expressed in Schema.org, primarily by one-to-one mappings or transparent lexical substitutions. Not only does this example support the argument that Schema.org is a reasonable starting point for a robust library resource description, but also that this solution is both a technical and a conceptual improvement. It is technically challenging to maintain URIs that make reference to a collection of namespaces, especially if they are defined in projects that primarily serve small, specialized academic communities, such as (de Melo 2014), whose long-term persistence cannot be guaranteed. Conceptually, it is difficult to interpret the true scope and intent of the British Library Data Model because the namespaces represent an ontological commitment to a large set of mature vocabularies and ontologies, which on close analysis might reveal untenable redundancies and semantic conflicts. Both of these problems are averted by adopting a single, more comprehensive standard—which, of course, did not exist when the British Library published their model and exists only partially now because Schema.org was not designed to serve the specialized needs of libraries.

OCLC's model of creative works has also been influenced by other emerging linked data standards and protocols. For example, the distinction between Work-as-Content and Work-as-Product can be broadly mapped to the BIBFRAME Work-Instance division (Godby 2013), which has been hailed as an improvement over models derived from a literal interpretation of the FRBR Group I hierarchy, because it eliminates distinctions that have proven especially difficult to discover algorithmically. But OCLC's model differs from BIBFRAME (LC 2014c) by placing a greater emphasis on modeling real-world objects for the purpose of discovery (Godby 2013; Godby and Denenberg 2015). The OCLC model of creative works has also been influenced by the draft W3C proposal for linking alternative representations of a document for discovery and fulfillment (Raman 2006). This protocol defines a generic information request that is fulfilled when the user specifies values for the language of the content, an edition identifier, and a file format appropriate for a particular rendering device. In our view, the abstract creative work corresponds to the generic information request, while the tangible versions of the creative work correspond to the document that is delivered. But the OCLC model differs from the Issue 53 protocol because it also accounts for the delivery of print materials and other physical objects.

3.4.6   THE OCLC MODEL OF WORKS: A SUMMARY

The most important pragmatic argument for basing the OCLC model on Schema.org is summarized in Chapter 1: that this is the vocabulary understood by the world's most important search engines. But another important reason is that Schema.org makes ontological sense. Since published books and other products of the human imagination are real-world objects, properties defined by third parties are understandable in the same way by members of the library community. Thus the Schema.org definitions of publisher, creator, ISBN, and nearly all of the other properties defined for Person, Organization, Place, and CreativeWork can be reused, eliminating the need to redefine these concepts in a specialized ontology that serves only the needs of libraries. Ever since Schema.org first appeared in 2011, we have believed that the vocabulary is incomplete rather than incorrect. But Schema.org is also growing rapidly. As we have shown, the addition of the GoodRelations ontology in 2013 has expanded the capacity of Schema.org to support enriched descriptions of library resources. The new accessibility features for CreativeWork and the recently announced taxonomy of Actions, which we have not yet had a chance to evaluate, may also be relevant to our goals. It is in the interest of the library standards community to monitor these developments because third parties may be doing much of the work that librarians had originally envisioned having to do themselves.

3.5   DISCOVERING CREATIVE WORKS THROUGH DATA MINING

In the rest of this chapter, we will briefly elaborate on a point that was first made in Chapter 1: that the RDF datasets being generated at OCLC is the result of a process that is far richer than the mapping of vocabulary from MARC to Schema.org and the newly defined terms available from extensions such as BiblioGraph.net. Instead, the goal is to build RDF datasets representing authoritative information about the six entities of interest in the current phase of our work—people, places, organizations, concepts, objects, and works—and define URIs that point to them. In this way, the knowledge locked in legacy metadata can be used to create next-generation library resource descriptions that are more machine-processable and project the expertise of librarianship outward to the broader Web. The evolving semantics of aggregations such as VIAF, described in Chapter 2, illustrate a path for moving forward with the development of authoritative resources for people, places, organizations, and concepts, since these entities fall within the scope of traditional library authority files.

Here we focus on Works—in particular, the distinctions defined in the FRBR Group I Model, and will describe the process of creating similar authoritative resources for these objects. The research described in Section 3.4 is the foundation for a workflow that discovers evidence in OCLC's legacy data stores for the new subclasses of schema:CreativeWork, creates RDF descriptions of them, and assigns the appropriate URI and RDF type. The data mining procedure is more complex because it not only evaluates the structured data of library records but is also beginning look further afield to semi-structured and unstructured text, which we describe in Chapter 4. In addition, the workflow accepts the large and growing corpus of WorldCat as input and supplements it with information available in the linked data versions of the authority files discussed in Chapter 2, which are also being iteratively improved. Some of the results are fed back to the authority files, ensuring that the Works algorithms operate on cleaner input in the next iteration.

Given that these procedures were first devised to improve the organization and display of library catalogs, the algorithms for identifying Works and Manifestations are the most mature. But research currently underway has already produced successful methods for identifying Expressions and Items, which promise to increase the quality as well as the scope of library metadata.

3.5.1   IDENTIFYING WORKS AND EXPRESSIONS

The algorithm for discovering Works in a corpus of MARC records is described in Hickey, O'Neill, and Toves (2002) and Hickey and Toves (2009), and has undergone continuous refinement as WorldCat has grown. But the fundamental procedure has remained the same. In the first step, authors, contributors, and titles are extracted from the MARC main entry and controlled access fields, normalized to a key, and assigned to a cluster that was produced in an earlier iteration. If the author-title key matches exactly with a previously processed key, it is assigned to the same Work cluster. If not, a controlled extended match consults the name and title variants available from the corresponding Work description maintained in VIAF, including translated forms of the title–creating, in effect a 'super'-Work from which Expression-like relationships can be derived. In the current version of the algorithm, subsequent processes identify only 'translation' relationships among the distinct creative works in this cluster, but other relationships are being studied. If all attempts at matching fail, a new Work cluster is created. In the second step of the algorithm, the Work clusters are mined to identify creators, secondary contributors, titles, description or summaries, and subjects. These processes are trivial if the Work cluster has only one record; and relatively straightforward if the cluster is large because the predominant values for these properties can be detected from simple frequency counts or counts weighted by library holdings. Work clusters are publishable only if they contain exactly one Work record from the previous iteration. Thus the algorithm is conservative and the residue requires human review.

As of April 2014, the Works clustering algorithm has been executed on about 80% of WorldCat without the need for extended matching. Among the millions of authors that can be extracted, fewer than 10,000 produce unstable results. But since these are the authors of the literary canon—William Shakespeare, Mark Twain, Anton Chekov, and others—whose names are controlled in authority files maintained by national libraries, this outcome can be translated into requirements for improving authority descriptions or aggregations such as VIAF. The run of the algorithm that generated the initial version of WorldCat Works dataset in April 2014 produced 194,928,712 clusters and 40,142,456, or 35%, contained more than one record. But these records are associated with nearly 75% of the holdings reported by the world's libraries. Thus the small subset of WorldCat for which Work clusters are meaningful is also the most visible.

3.5.2   IDENTIFYING MANIFESTATIONS AND ITEMS

When the FRBR Group I model was formulated in the 1990s, a MARC record accessible from an online catalog or an aggregate such as WorldCat was commonly interpreted as a Manifestation. The same interpretation is shared by metadata standards experts in the publishing community, who aligned Manifestation with Product, the top-level term in the ONIX specification, which was being developed at the same time as the FRBR model (Bell 2012). Since ONIX influenced the design of schema:CreativeWork, it is not surprising that Manifestations can be described in Schema.org with little need to define extensions.

In the linked data projects we have described in this book, a Manifestation is connected through the schema:workExample property to a Work, as shown in Figure 3.6 for *Joy of Cooking*. Yet an examination of the linked data shown in the inset reveals that the description is associated not with a Manifestation identifier, but with a WorldCat URL—in other words, a noisy surrogate for a Manifestation entity, which can be identified only by a clustering algorithm. If each bibliographic record contained only a single ISBN or other product identifier, no such computation would be necessary. But the publishing industry does not guarantee a one-to-one mapping between identical products and ISBNs because a single product may have more than one ISBN as the publisher supply chain moves from the assignment of ten-digit to thirteen-digit codes; conversely, multiple products may have the same ISBN as publishers address the issue of whether identical content delivered as a hardback book or an e-book requires separate identifiers (Dawson 2012).

The other problem is that WorldCat is an aggregation of collaboratively contributed records, which means that it contains multiple descriptions of the same object or class of objects. Though duplicate detection algorithms can detect the most obvious redundancies, a deeper analysis is required to detect others, especially when the languages of description are different. This problem was defined by (Gatenby et al. 2012). An example from their analysis showing some of the details that must be reconciled is reproduced in Figure 3.13, which contains excerpts from a German-language and an English-language MARC record describing the same book, *Grosse Naturforscher: Geschichte der Naturforschung in Lebensbeschreibungen*. A human reader can verify that these are descriptions of the same book because the title, author, publisher, and publication dates are the same, though the corresponding string values do not match exactly. The physical descriptions are also exactly the same, once an algorithm has been informed that '332 p.' and '332 S.' are equivalent because 'Seite' is the German word for 'pages.' The physical measurements are also the same because 8 inches equal 22 centimeters.

100 1 $a Lenard, Philipp, $d 1862-1947.	100 1 $a Lenard, Philipp.
245 10 $a Grosse Naturforscher : $b eine Geschichte der Naturforschung in Lebensbeschreibungen / $c von Philipp Lenard.	245 10 $a Große Naturforscher: $b eine Geschichte der Naturforschung in Lebensbeschreibungen / $c von Philipp Lenard.
	250 $a 2., verm. Aufl.
260 $a München : $b J.F. Lehmann, $c 1930.	260 $a München: $b Lehmann, $c 1930.
300 $a 332 p. : $b ill., ports. ; $c 22cm	330 $a 332 S: $b Ill; $c 8°

Figure 3.13: Descriptions of the same book in two languages (Gatenby et al. 2012).

A process that collects such observations into a set of heuristics has been deployed on portions of WorldCat and only minor upgrades are required to assign Manifestation identifiers to the results. As the Gatenby, et al., study shows, these heuristics also improve the Work cluster algorithm because they consider a broader range of data, permitting the assignment of records to Work clusters that are missed when data associated only with authors, titles, and uniform titles is considered.

The only remaining FRBR category is the Item, about which we have little to report because the management of items is traditionally done by libraries, not aggregators such as OCLC. From a data processing perspective, it is obvious that Items present the same problems as Manifestations because aggregations such as WorldCat have multiple descriptions of the same thing, often in different languages. But before addressing this problem, we need to develop a taxonomy of what an Item can be and how various descriptions relate to it, which is the subject of a research project on aggregated descriptions of cultural heritage materials in discussed in Chapter 4. An added benefit is that the consideration of Items moves the discussion beyond the stewardship of published materials to archives, special collections, and digitized objects—resources that may someday comprise the largest segment of library collections. This focus might be expected to expose inadequacies in a model derived from an ontology designed to facilitate the movement of products in a marketplace, but we are optimistic that Schema.org is up to the task. Chapter 5 presents a sketch of a model for digital objects, an extension of the model described in this chapter. Once implemented, such a model could expose the availability of unique items held by libraries to the broader Web, perhaps through the model for library holdings that has already been developed.

3.6   CHAPTER SUMMARY

This chapter completes the description, started in Chapter 2, of the semantic model that underlies the network of statements published as RDFa on bibliographic records accessible from World-Cat.org. Though it is an early draft, the process flow successfully creates machine-understandable statements about key entities— persons, organizations, places, topics, works, and objects— that populate the largest corpus of bibliographic descriptions managed by the library community. It is now possible to make subtle but sophisticated assertions about the domain of library resource management such as 'A 1997 edition of *Joy of Cooking*, a book written by Irma von Starkloff Rombauer, is available for lending at the Grandview Public Library' or 'An edition of *The Snow Queen*, published in 1987 by North-South Books, is an English translation of the German translation *Schneekönigin*, which is translated from the Danish original *Snedronnigen* written by Hans-Christian Andersen.'

For the first time, such statements can be formulated in terms that are comprehensible to general-purpose search engines and other data consumers outside the library community. They are unambiguous and trustworthy because text strings such as 'Hans Christian Andersen' have been upgraded to resolvable references to real-world objects—or more idiomatically, 'things'—and replaced with persistent, globally unique identifiers such as `http://viaf.org/viaf/4925902`, which point to machine-understandable hubs of authoritative information managed by the library community and affiliated professionals.

Chapter 2 argues that library authority files are realistic predecessors to the authoritative hubs seemingly required by the conventions that make up the linked data paradigm. Authoritative hubs for creative works defined with the different levels of concreteness or specificity in the FRBR Group I hierarchy are also required for addressing the most important use case for linked data in the domain of libraries and librarianship: facilitating the discovery and delivery of the resources that satisfy the information needs of the public. But hubs for creative works have no direct antecedent in legacy standards or data stores and must be generated from algorithms operating on bibliographic descriptions.

The first result is WorldCat Works, which contains globally persistent URIs for nearly 200 million Works that resolve to descriptions modeled in Schema.org. They are automatically derived from WorldCat catalog records using algorithms developed by OCLC researchers working on the empirical discovery of the FRBR conceptual model in collections of bibliographic descriptions maintained by libraries. Though WorldCat Works is still experimental, its significance is already being recognized. For example, linked data experts at the Library of Congress have acknowledged that WorldCat Works are compatible with BIBFRAME Works and plan to include WorldCat Work URIs in future BIBFRAME descriptions (Godby and Denenberg 2015). Researchers participating in the 'Linked Data for Libraries' (or LD4L) project, expect to do the same. LD4L is a joint project led by libraries at Cornell, Harvard, and Stanford Universites and funded by the Institute for Library and Museum Studies, or IMLS (2015). The anticipated outcome is a set of cross-references among items in the collections held at the three participating institutions where none existed before (LD4L 2015a). When the results of these experiments become available, WorldCat Works can be evaluated as a collection point for links in the Semantic Web, a concept we introduced in Chapter 1. If the promise of linked data is upheld, the outcome should be greater visibility for libraries and their contents on the Web. Increased click-through rates to libraries that correlate with the inclusion of Work URIs in the RDF statements published on WorldCat.org have already been reported (Fons 2015).

Nevertheless, the results described in this chapter are a baseline and a proof of concept, a demonstration of a draft model and a set of machine-understandable statements that can be discovered in over 300 million legacy bibliographic records. But the model, as well as the processes that discover evidence for it in legacy data, are positioned for rapid maturation. Chapter 4 describes algorithms that consider a broader range of evidence for the entities and relationships that populate the resources managed by libraries. So far, the development of models has focused on monographs, but projects are already underway that expand their scope to include digital objects, the contents of institutional repositories, and electronic journal articles. Some of these projects are mentioned in Chapter 5. In addition, our collaboration with the Library of Congress is enhancing the interoperability of OCLC's linked data models with BIBFRAME. This work aims to strike a balance between description and discovery, which recognizes the professional cataloger's requirement for scholarly detail and precision, while making the case that much of the domain of library resource description is comprehensible to the information-seeking public and useful in the broader Web.

Linked data representations of creative works representing the perspective of librarianship have come a long way in just three and a half years, when the authors of the W3C-sponsored *Library Linked Data Incubator Group Final Report* could document only modest progress on this difficult problem. A plausible direction is now clear, and many of the issues that must still be addressed are well understood.

CHAPTER 4

Entity Identification Through Text Mining

4.1 THE NEED

Throughout this book, we have emphasized two stubborn facts about legacy library data: it consists primarily of human-readable text that is difficult for machines to process, and the reliable structured data that served as input to the first-generation linked data models is severely restricted. Put in more colloquial terms, library linked data models have been built by picking low-hanging fruit, primarily from the controlled access fields of MARC bibliographic records and their corresponding associations with library authority files. This has been a productive strategy, yielding globally unique URIs for four of the six key entities—people, places, organizations, and concepts—that frame the scope of our investigation, as well as the first drafts of authoritative hubs derived from library authority files and a concrete list of tasks for achieving greater maturity. But Chapter 3 showed the need to go beyond controlled-access fields to assemble the evidence required for building authoritative hubs of creative works. The need is especially acute because the algorithms that produce the outputs required by the linked data paradigm are built on older processes designed to identify semantically important similarities or to eliminate errors and redundancies in conventionally designed aggregations of library resource descriptions—problems that must also be addressed in the management of WorldCat cataloging data as well as other collections such as Europeana (2014) and the Digital Public Library of America (DPLA 2014). But these processes are reaching their upper limits, and we are now evaluating the algorithms developed by text mining researchers.

4.1.1 TEXT MINING DEFINED

Rooted in computational linguistics and information retrieval (Hearst 1999), text mining—also known as intelligent text analysis, text data mining, or knowledge-discovery in text—refers to the process of discovering and capturing semantic information and knowledge from large collections of unstructured text. The ultimate goal is to enable knowledge discovery via either textual or visual access for use in a wide range of significant applications. It is different from data mining, which is more about discovering patterns in numeric or structured data stored in databases. Though similar techniques are sometimes used, text mining has many additional constraints caused by the unstructured nature of the textual content and the use of natural languages. It uses techniques from information retrieval, information extraction, and natural language processing and connects them with the algorithms and methods of knowledge discovery in databases, data mining, machine learning and statistics.

4.1.2   ASSOCIATING TEXT WITH A URI

The data problems that we address using text mining algorithms are both easier and more challenging to solve than those encountered in unstructured free text, the typical input to text mining algorithms that have been studied in the computer science and computational linguistics research communities.

On the one hand, the problems in the domain of library resource management are easier to solve because library metadata is semi-structured. For example, entity recognition algorithms have relatively little work to do in a string such as 'Publisher: Washington, DC; Potomac Books, 2005' because the text is sparse, the punctuation identifies important phrase boundaries, and the string is already labeled with the name of an important relationship—namely, 'Publisher', from which a software process can infer that the name of a person or organization can be found somewhere in the rest of the text. Moreover, WorldCat, like most aggregations of library resource descriptions, contains a large amount of highly curated, structured data that can already be correctly associated through an algorithmic process with the entities and relationships in a linked data model, as we have argued. This substrate of clean data can be used to bootstrap information discovery in data elsewhere in WorldCat that is much more difficult to process.

But our needs are demanding because the outputs of text mining algorithms are useful only if they meet high standards for accuracy in a large-scale production environment. As we follow Coyle's prescription (Coyle 2012) for preparing library resource descriptions for input into a linked data model of library resource description, we are ascending a staircase, moving from free text to normalized text to data associated with dereferenceable URIs. If this information can be correctly extracted, labeled, linked with named properties, and aggregated with third-party resources, text mining algorithms can populate our model and be used to discover previously undetected patterns, maps of connections, and trends. But these algorithms eventually produce diminishing returns when they operate on data that is too sparse and full of errors.

The unifying goal of the research projects described in this chapter is to extract data from the text in OCLC's collections and advance it toward a fully articulated linked data representation. In the sections below, we identify three important needs by the work presented in previous chapters and show how the most relevant text mining sub-disciplines can be used to address them.

4.2   RECOGNIZING KEY ENTITIES

The discussion can begin by considering the MARC record shown in Figure 4.1, which is a complete excerpt for the coded data fields numbered below 245. This is a description of a book about local history compiled by the Little River County Historical Society in Arkansas. It is represented by two records available from WorldCat—one with the publisher Heritage House Publishers and the other shown below, which lists the publisher as Heritage House Pub. Copies of books matching both descriptions are available from libraries in Fort Wayne, Indiana; Independence, Missouri; and Little Rock, Pine Bluff, and Bentonville, Arkansas.

245 02 $a A history of Ashdown, Arkansas / $c compiled by the Little River County Historical Society.
260 __ $a Marceline, MO : $b Heritage House Pub., $c c2006.
300 __ $a v, 203 p. : $b ill., maps ; $c 29 cm.
500 __ $a Includes index of names.
520 __ $a Much of the information included (1836-2006) is derived from Little River News articles, Bill Beasley's History of Littler River County, interviews with residents who provided photos and documents, and from Judge John C. Finley III, who began to research the history of this town in 1992.
651 _0 $a Ashdown (Ark.) $x History.
651 _0 $a Arkansas $z Ashdown $x Genealogy.
651 _0 $a Little River County (Ark.) $v History.
710 2_ $a Little River County Historical Society (Ark.)

Figure 4.1: A MARC record describing a work of local American history. WorldCat ID 144513901.

The RDF/Turtle representation published on WorldCat.org is shown in Figure 4.2. Note that only two of the RDF objects are represented as URIs. Two schema:about statements correctly mention the identifiers for 'Arkansas—Little River County' and 'Arkansas.'

But most of the other objects in the RDF/Turtle representation are represented as strings, including several key entities, such as the name of the publisher and the name of the corporate author 'Little River County Historical Society.' Several subject headings also lack URIs, such as 'Ashdown (Ark.)' and 'Little River County (Ark.)' which to a human reader appears to refer to the same place as the heading associated with the FAST URI http://id.worldcat.org/fast/1217655 ('Arkansas—Little River County'). In addition, the description mentions other entities, such as the related work 'History of Little River County,' the organization named 'Little River News,' and 'Judge John C. Finley III,' who contributed to the history of Ashdown described in the MARC record.

The goal of several research projects now being conducted at OCLC is to promote strings to entities by applying text mining algorithms to MARC records and other library resource descriptions represented in text-heavy legacy formats. Schematically, Figure 4.3 represents the population of nameable entities in a large aggregated database of library resource descriptions such as WorldCat. The concentric circles can be read as slices of a three-dimensional solid representing increasingly larger segments of an information space containing entities with potentially assignable identifiers.

Chapter 2 showed that an identifier is assignable only if the string appears in a controlled MARC field and the controlling authority has been modeled as linked data, which means that

```
<http://www.worldcat.org/oclc/401008804>
a schema:Book ;
    schema:name "A history of Ashdown, Arkansas" ;
    schema:contributor [a schema:Organization "Little River County Historical Society
(Ark.)"] ;
    schema:publisher [a schema:Organization schema:name "Heritage House Publishers"] ;
    library:placeOfPublication [a schema:Place schema:name "Marceline, MO"] ;
    schema:about <http://id.worldcat.org/fast/1217655> ;
    schema:about <http://id.worldcat.org/fast/1204809> ;
    schema:about
        [a schema:Place; schema:Name "Little River County (Ark.)"] ;
    schema:about
        [a schema:Place; schema:Name "Ashdown (Ark.)"] ;
    schema:description "Much of the information included (1836-2006) is derived from Little
River News articles, Bill Beasley's History of Littler River County, interviews with residents
who provided photos and documents, and from Judge John C. Finley III, who began to
research the history of this town in 1992." ;
    schema:exampleOfWork <http://worldcat.org/entity/work/id/103221012> .
```

Figure 4.2: RDF/Turtle for the corresponding Schema.org markup.

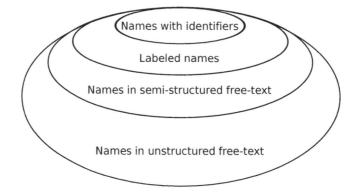

Figure 4.3: Sources of named entities in a corpus of bibliographic metadata.

identifiers for people, organizations, concepts, and topics have effectively been established by a long process initiated by the spadework of human catalogers. They form the smallest segment on the top of Figure 4.3.

The second segment represents the population of entities that have already been labeled by catalogers as persons, places, organizations, or concepts, but are not associated with identifiers, such as the publisher ('Heritage House Pub.'), the place of publication ('Marceline, MO'), and the contributor ('Little River County Historical Society, Ark.') of the example shown in Figure 4.1. Most importantly, this subset of entities have key relationships to the creative work, such as publisher, author, contributor, and 'aboutness.' In many cases, these entities can be associated with identifiers already defined in library authority files or third-party resources such as DBpedia or Geonames. And once these strings are promoted to entities, further improvements to the description should be possible. For example, it will be obvious that the description contains two mentions of the place with the name 'Little River County (Ark.)' in the list of schema:about statements, one of which could be eliminated. It is therefore critical for the prospects of the large-scale conversion of WorldCat catalog records to linked data that entity-recognition algorithms consider an expanded body of evidence because less robust methods are already nearing their upper limits.

In Section 4.2.2, we will discuss the third segment: free text that is highly structured or stylized, to which named-entity extraction algorithms can be productively applied. Some of the extracted entities have assignable identifiers, but many do not. The final segment represents unstructured free text such as texts marked up with schema:description in Figure 4.2, which is the typical input to natural language processing algorithms studied by academic computer science or information science researchers. Since here the entity extraction and identity resolution tasks are the most challenging, we will address them only after some of the more tractable problems have been solved.

The text mining solution most relevant here is named entity recognition, or NER, a well-studied set of software processes developed in the academic computing community for identifying atomic elements in a string and labeling them with the names of predefined categories for people, places, organizations, and concepts (Godby et al. 2010). But despite the obvious overlap between the names of the key entities in OCLC's linked data model and those labeled by NER tools, the fit is only approximate. As the examples below demonstrate, the most important requirement for success in the string-to-thing promotion task, at least as we have defined it, is the presence of relevant machine-processable data elsewhere in the record, such as coded or controlled data and previously assigned identifiers. A process involving NER may exploit this information, but it is only one tool among many that is useful for addressing this problem.

4.2.1   LABELED NAMES

As mentioned, these names have already been labeled by human catalogers but have not been subjected to authority control and can only be mapped to string values in the current Schema.org markup published on WorldCat.org. In words that might be used by an natural language processing researcher, the entity has been extracted but not disambiguated. But the locations of these names in a MARC record imply that they represent key entities with machine-processable relationships to creative works. At the very least, this information can be used to construct RDF triples represented by the pseudo-code <'A History of Ashdown'> <Publisher> <'Heritage House Publishers'>, to use data from the record cited above.

Publishers

Figure 4.4 contains a truncated MARC record accessible from WorldCat that describes *Clean Your Room, Harvey Moon!*—a first-grade primer published in New York, presumably for an audience of American schoolchildren. As in previously discussed examples, Pat Cummings, the primary author, is listed in the authority-controlled 100 field and is thus associated with a VIAF identifier in the corresponding Schema.org markup. But the 260 field mentions the names of two additional entities—'New York' and 'Macmillan/McGraw-Hill School Pub. Co.'—which are also important in the domain of library resource description but have not been subjected to authority control. The semantics of the MARC record identify the first as the name of a place, which is related to the creative work with the OCLC-defined property library:placeOfPublication, which is slated to be redefined in BiblioGraph. The second is the name of an organization, which is related to the creative work with the property schema:publisher. This markup is visible in the RDF statements accessible from WorldCat.org, as we have noted in the discussion of similar examples in earlier chapters.

100 1_	$a Cummings, Pat
245	$a Clean your room, Harvey Moon! $c by Pat Cummings.
260	$a New York : $b Macmillan/McGraw-Hill School Pub. Co., $c1993
490	$a Macmillan/McGraw-Hill reading/language arts. New view. Grade one
650 _0	$a Readers (Primary)
650 _7	$a Readers (Primary) $2 fast
710 2_	$a Macmillan/McGraw-Hill School Publishing Company

Figure 4.4: A MARC record with controlled and uncontrolled names. WorldCat ID 28284368.

Special processing is required to promote the two strings mentioned in the MARC 260 field to identifiers, despite the fact that URIs are available for both entities: in VIAF for the publisher, and in FAST and LCSH for the place of publication. To associate the names with the URIs, it is necessary to devise a process that matches the two strings to a skos:prefLabel or skos:altLabel listed in the corresponding SKOS-encoded authority-file description of the concept, a format discussed in Chapter 2. But since the two strings do not appear in the MARC description in an authority-controlled field, they may vary from the authoritative source because of spelling or transcription errors or differences in local descriptive practice. The association of the string 'New York' with the correct identifier might appear relatively straightforward because this well-known geographic name can be interpreted by a human reader of the MARC record shown in Figure 4.4 as the name of the city in the state of New York. Real-world knowledge fills in the gap that 'place of publication' in a bibliographic description usually involves the mention of a major international city where publication houses are located, such as New York, New York; London, England; or Tokyo, Japan; but not London, Ohio, a farming village in central Ohio. But the knowledge was not available to the machine process that produced the microdata for WorldCat and 'New York' is marked up as a string instead of an entity.

Unfortunately, no URI was assigned to the publisher name at all because such names are typically not controlled in library authority files. Publishing companies are so frequently reorganized that considerable human effort is required to maintain a resource that tracks the history of organizations such as Macmillan and McGraw-Hill, which were once separate companies but have recently been merged to form a single company with the name 'Macmillan/McGraw-Hill' (Connaway and Dickey 2011). But even if this resource is created, it is difficult to establish the correct form of the name because the publishing industry does not maintain its own authority files.

Nevertheless, the presence of the 710 field in the above figure promises to solve part of the problem. Perhaps because elementary-school primers often have corporate authors, a string containing the words 'Macmillan/McGraw-Hill' is available as a controlled name, reflecting the fact that this company has been attested as a creator or contributor to a creative work. Most publishers do not receive this treatment because they do not typically act as authors. But if present, the 710 field permits the inference that the string has been defined in the Library of Congress Name Authority File, from which a VIAF identifier can be algorithmically derived, while the 260 field supplements the description with the fact that this corporate entity has a 'publisher' relationship to the creative work. A fuzzy matching algorithm applied to the MARC record would be required to associate the strings appearing in the 260 and 710 fields. This heuristic would have a reasonable chance of being successful, but to ensure that the name is correct, timely, and close to the form of the name that is prevalent in the publisher supply chain, more robust text mining algorithms would be required to build an authoritative resource of publisher names or match them with existing identifiers registered with ISNI (2014). OCLC researchers are currently investigating this possibility.

Translators

In the Multilingual WorldCat study first mentioned in Chapter 3 (Gatenby 2013), one important task is the identification of translators in MARC bibliographic records. If one book is a translation of another, the cataloger should indicate the name of the translator in the $a subfield and the 'translator' role in the $e ('Relator Term') or $4 ('Relator Code') subfields of the MARC 700 field. When this data is present, it can be transformed directly into linked data, which was done for more than 65,000 records in the 'data.bnf.fr' project (Simon et al. 2013). But in WorldCat catalog data, the subfields $e and $4 for the 100/700 fields are sparsely populated. Only 45 million (14%) records in WorldCat have been cataloged with $e or $4, and only a subset of these, or 1.6 million records, make explicit mention of translators. Thus if we only rely on machine-processable metadata, most of the translators would be missed, in part because cataloging rules do not require authority control for translators.

100 1_ $a Ao Si Ding $c (Austen, Jane, 1775-1817)

245 10 $a Ao man yu pian jian = $b Pride and prejudice / $c Zhen. ao si ting zhu ; Li shu zhen yi.

260 __ $aTai bei shi : $b Xing yue wen hua chu ban ; $a Tai bei xian shu lin shi : $b Cheng yang zong dai li, $c 2002[min 91]

700 1_ $a Li, Shu-zhen $c (ying yu)

700 1_ $a Austen, Jane, $d 1775-1817.

880 1_ $6 100-02/$1 $a 奥斯丁 $c (Austen, Jane, 1775-1817)

880 10 $6 245-03/$1 $a 傲慢與偏見 = $b Pride and prejudice / $c 珍.奥斯汀著 ; 李淑貞譯

880 1_ $6 700-09/$1 $a 李淑貞 $c (英語)

Figure 4.5: Identifying translators in 245$c. WorldCat ID 301886026.

100 1_ $a Cao, Xueqin, $d approximately 1717-1763.

240 10 $a Hong lou meng. $l English

245 14 $a The dream of the red chamber $h [electronic resource] : $b Hung lou meng, books I and II / $c Cao Xueqin ; translated by H. Bencraft Joly.

260 __ $a [S.l.] : $b Duke Classics, $c c2012.

700 1_ $a Joly, H. Bencraft.

Figure 4.6: Identifying translators in 245$c. WorldCat ID 795566543.

100 1_ $a Wu, Cheng'en, $d approximately 1500-approximately 1582.

240 10 $a Xiyou ji. $l French

245 13 $a La Pérégrination vers l'Ouest = $b (Xiyou ji) / $c Wu Cheng'en ; texte traduit, présenté et annoté par André Leévy.

260 __ $a [Paris] : $b Gallimard, $c 1991.

700 1_ $a Lévy, André.

Figure 4.7: Identifying translators in 245$c. WorldCat ID 24814406.

A more careful look at the metadata reveals that the translators are often indicated in the free-text 245$c ('Statement of Responsibility') field, as shown in Figures 4.5, 4.6, and 4.7. Human readers can easily detect that 'Li shu zhen,' 'H. Bencraft Joly,' and 'Leévy, André' are translators, indicated by 'yi' (and 譯 meaning 'translate' in Chinese in the 800-245$c field), 'translated by' and 'traduit' ('translated' in French) in the free-text 245$c field, highlighted in red. Though these names are cataloged in the authority-controlled 700 field, their relationships to the corresponding Works are unknown. As a result, these names can be labeled only as schema:Contributor instead of a more precise property. Since their appearance in the 700 fields permits them to be labeled as personal names, they could be assigned VIAF identifiers with high confidence,[1] or they could be added into VIAF through a semi-automated process.

As in the case of publisher names, a text mining approach could be applied here to match the personal names in the controlled 700 field with the names in the free text of the 245$c field, with the help of a list of words that indicate translators in different languages and writing systems (such as 'translated by,' 译 or 譯 (Chinese), 'traduit' (French), 'traducción' (Spanish), etc.). In this way, more translator entities could be detected. Our current text mining software has successfully detected translators for an extra 2.7 million records.

However, matching these names requires a more complex process than simple string matching. The names occurring in the 245$c field often have different forms from those in the 700 field—for example, 'H. Bencraft Joly' vs. 'Joly, H. Bencraft.' For non-Latin scripts, such as Chinese, Japanese, and Korean names, matching based on their romanized characters is not reliable; instead, the matching needs to be done on characters in their original scripts cataloged in the 880 fields (see Figure 4.5). Furthermore, translators could be introduced in different ways in free text, such as the example shown in Figure 4.7. Matching the correct name string and identifying its role is therefore not as straightforward as it appeared in the beginning, and the task of matching these name strings with the correct names in VIAF is an additional challenge.

More often than not, the name of a translator is never explicitly cataloged in the controlled 700 field and is only mentioned in the free-text 245$c field. These names belong to the bottom segment in Figure 4.3 and require a more sophisticated extraction process from unstructured text. But the data obtained from the matching of the 700 and corresponding 245$c fields can be used as a training set for an entity-extraction classifier to extract translators in the 245$c field. However, because of the complexity and variation observed in natural-language free text, a completely automated solution to this problem is unlikely, and a hybrid approach that combines machine learning with crowdsourcing by librarians or domain experts is probably more practical.

4.2.2 NAMES IN SEMI-STRUCTURED TEXT

As shown in previous chapters, MARC records that contain relatively little unstructured text are easily rendered as RDF triples. But some cataloging communities make extensive use of highly formatted notes featuring many entities and relationships. We are exploring the possibility that this text could be promoted to a more machine-processable format. Figure 4.8 shows an excerpt of a MARC record available from WorldCat describing a film about Rodgers and Hammerstein, the team that created many famous Broadway musicals, including *The King and I, Oklahoma!*, and *The Sound of Music*.

A human reader can discern that the MARC 245 field mentions both important names in the 'Title' string. But the 600 fields supplied by the cataloger do the real work of establishing the connection with the real-world entities. The semantics of the MARC 600 field permit the inference that the creative work with the title *Richard Rodgers and Oscar Hammerstein, II* is indeed

---

1. 'H. Bencraft Joly' and 'Lévy, André' indeed have VIAF identifiers while 'Li shu zhen' does not.

245         $a Richard Rodgers and Oscar Hammerstein, II.
490         $a American musical theatre.
508         $a script, Edith Hall; editor, Fay Davidson; illustrator, Richard Hall; producer, Brenda Herz; director, Karen Weintraub.
600 10 $a Rodgers, Richard, $d 1902-1979
600 10 $a Hammerstein, Oscar, $d 1895-1960

[[Role script] [Person Edith Hall]]
[[Role editor] [Person Fay Davidson]]
[[Role illustrator] [Person Richard Hall]]
[[Role producer] [Person Brenda Herz]]

Figure 4.8: Extractable named entities and roles in a MARC record for a film. WorldCat ID 2692124.

'about' two unique individuals whose names are controlled in the Library of Congress Name Authority file. As we have seen, the presence of a controlled access point in a MARC description also enables the assignment of a VIAF identifier. Thus, the strings 'Richard Rodgers' and 'Oscar Hammerstein' have been identified and disambiguated through the normal course of cataloging, and have been associated with resolvable identifiers through mature linked data models of library authority files.

The MARC 508 field is a formatted note containing names of other people and the roles they performed in the creation and production of the film. Though the data in this field is a long string whose contents are accessible in WorldCat only through keyword indexing, a human reader can easily parse the names and roles into the list shown below the excerpted record. This is also the output that could be obtained from an named-entity extractor enhanced with the ability to identify the names of roles in this limited context. Since the information shown in the MARC 508 field in Figure 4.8 is both valuable and within the scope of what named-entity extractors enhanced with heuristics that identify the names of roles in this limited context could compute with reasonable accuracy, we are investigating the feasibility of mining all 6.3 million records in WorldCat that describe films or recordings of theatrical and musical performances to extract names and roles from formatted MARC notes fields. Using information available elsewhere in the record, an algorithm would transform the data to RDF triples such as <Richard Hall> <illustrator> <Richard Rodgers and Oscar Hammerstein, II>. Roles such as 'illustrator' or 'director' are valuable for producing richer RDF statements, as they introduce more real-world relations between people and creative works.

Current results on a small pilot study show accuracy rates nearing 88% for the extraction of names and 75% for roles. If the results can be replicated on a larger sample, this project promises to yield a large and heretofore unexplored network of names and relationships in the domain of musical and theatrical performance contributed by multiple communities of specialized library catalogers. But several challenges must be overcome. First, notes fields are still free text, even if they are highly formatted, and not all of the 508 fields attested in WorldCat conform to easily discovered patterns. Second, a full resolution of this problem awaits results from the research on multilingual bibliographic descriptions discussed above, partly because some of the text is not in English and partly because VIAF descriptions will have to be created for some of the extracted names using the same conventions. Finally, an extra interpretation step is required to transform the names of roles such as 'script' discovered in the text to a more precise property of agency, such as 'script writer.' Nevertheless, in a corpus as large as WorldCat, even a subset of correctly parsed data contains information that can be channeled to upstream processes, and we are devising algorithms that can identify these results automatically.

4.2.3   NAMES IN UNSTRUCTURED TEXT

Though it is outside the scope of our current work, the processing of names found in unstructured text, depicted schematically as the lowest segment of Figure 4.3, is a potentially rewarding task because it promises to reveal even richer knowledge from the legacy data contributed by library catalogers from all over the world. For example, the short summary shown in Figure 4.1 connects at least two published books and their authors, a local organization, and an event involving a judge researching local history. This is an interesting piece of real-world knowledge hidden in a single bibliographic record. Though current state-of-the-art NER tools cannot extract the named entities with the precision required for library resource description, such knowledge could be extracted with the help of local history enthusiasts or other specialized communities, a strategy that is already being pursued in the library community. For example, the 'Linked Jazz' project sponsored by the New York Public Library has successfully engaged a community of popular jazz enthusiasts to annotate the names and relationships among artists, performers, and musical works in a corpus of digitized documents, which have been converted to RDF triples (Pattuelli et al. 2013).

4.3   CONCEPT MATCHING

Persons, organizations, and places are key entities in the initial draft of OCLC's linked data model of resources managed by libraries, but so are concepts or subjects. Libraries use controlled knowledge organization systems (KOSs), such as thesauri or subject heading lists (SHLs), to describe the subjects of the records in their collections. KOSs are typically stored as Name Authority records in MARC 21 name authority files, as we discussed in Chapter 2 (Section 2.2.1). Following the standard set by LCSH, library standards experts have modeled many name authority files in SKOS (see Section 2.2.2), where a skos:Concept is a curated string with an implied meaning defined by its position in a thesaurus. A richer set of links among the concepts defined in these authority files would improve access to individual resource descriptions and realize part of the vision that motivates the development of linked data: greater visibility for libraries in the global web of data.

Concept matching also solves more immediate problems. When bibliographic records are aggregated, de-duplicated, and merged into aggregations such as the WorldCat database, many records end up with subjects from multiple authority files, often expressed in different languages. Figure 4.9 shows an example. The topical subjects in three different colors are from English, Dutch, and French thesauri, respectively. The English subjects are from LCSH and refer to concepts defined in an authority file that has already been modeled as linked data. However, the Dutch and French subjects are defined in GTT and Répertoire de vedettes-matière, which are still represented in legacy record formats, and are therefore represented only as strings, not URIs, in the RDF markup published on WorldCat.org. But a more careful look at these fields reveals that the French subjects are literal translations of the English ones, consisting primarily of cognates that are obvious even to readers who do not know French. The Dutch subjects are also synonymous to the English concepts to readers who understand Dutch: 'Letterkunde' (Literature), 'Engles' (English), 'Godsdienst' (Religion), and 'Victoriaanse tijd' (Victorian era). None of the corresponding terms are connected by machine-processable assertions of relatedness.

100 1_	$a Oulton, Carolyn, $d 1972-	
245 10	$a Literature and religion in mid-Victorian England : $b from Dickens to Eliot / $c Carolyn W. de la L. Oulton.	
260 __	$a New York : $b Palgrave Macmillan, $c 2003.	
650 _0	$a English fiction $y 19th century $x History and criticism.	
650 _0	$a Christianity and literature $z England $x History $y 19th century.	
650 _0	$a Religion and literature $z England $x History $y 19th century.	
650 _0	$a Christian fiction, English $x History and criticism.	
650 _0	$a Religion in literature.	
650 17	$a Letterkunde. $2 gtt	
650 17	$a Engels. $2 gtt	
650 17	$a Godsdienst. $2 gtt	
650 17	$a Victoriaanse tijd. $2 gtt	
650 _6	$a Roman anglais $y 19e siècle $x Histoire et critique.	
650 _6	$a Christianisme et littératur $z Angleterre $x Histoire $y 19e siècle.	
650 _6	$a Religion et littératur $z Angleterre $x Hi. stoire $y 19e siècle.	
650 _6	$a Roman chrétien anglais $x Histoire et critique.	
650 _6	$a Religion dans la littératur.	

Figure 4.9: A MARC record with multilingual subjects from three different thesauri. WorldCat ID 49902891.

If the concepts were mapped, the description could be customized to the user's language of choice and the display would appear less cluttered because English users would see only the heading 'Religion in literature,' not the apparently redundant French heading 'Religion et littératur.'

As an added benefit, users who issue subject searches could retrieve results in a different language from that of their query, overcoming barriers to access that occur when a library collection is described in the local language regardless of the language of the content. For example, consider the monolingual English-speaking user living in Paris who is interested in books about sprinting. Since books held by the Bibliothèque nationale de France are most likely described with a French thesaurus, books about sprinting would be assigned the subject heading 'Course de vitesse' ('sprinting' in French), and the user's query 'Sprinting' would be unsuccessful even if the collection has an English-language book on this topic. But the request could be fulfilled if the French thesaurus were modeled in SKOS with an owl:sameAs or skos:closeMatch property that links the French skos:Concept to the corresponding English one, as shown in Figure 4.10. An automated process could then follow such links to retrieve books with the same or closely matched subjects.

```
<http://data.bnf.fr/ark:/12148/cb12544657q>
a skos:Concept ;
    skos:prefLabel "Course de vitesse"@fr ;
    skos:altLabel "100 mètres (athlétisme)"@fr,
        "200 mètres (athlétisme)"@fr,
        "400 mètres (athlétisme)"@fr,
        "Cent mètres plat"@fr,
        "Courses de vitesse"@fr,
        "Sprint (athlétisme)"@fr,
        "Vitesse (athlétisme)"@fr ;
    skos:closeMatch <http://d-nb.info/gnd/4166247-7>,
        <http://d-nb.info/gnd/4188278-7>,
        <http://d-nb.info/gnd/4191233-0>,
        <http://dewey.info/class/793/>,
        <http://id.loc.gov/authorities/sh85127031#concept> .
```

Figure 4.10: One Rameau concept is linked to concepts from three other thesauri.

As we will show below, an aggregation of metadata about creative works such as World-Cat can be consulted as a corpus by an automated process to obtain evidence for the owl:sameAs or skos:closeMatch relationships, which can then be algorithmically applied to the corresponding authority files.

4.3.1   CREATING ALIGNMENTS

While much manual effort has been undertaken to create alignments, or sets of mappings (Landry 2009), a crucial problem with this approach is its enormous cost. Some reports mention that around 90 terms may be matched per day by a skilled information professional dealing with concepts in the same language (Will 2001); but in a multilingual context, the rate is lower. Automated matching methods are clearly necessary.

Semantic Web research is identifying the similarities and differences between the task of matching controlled vocabularies and the more generic task of ontology matching (Shvaiko and Euzenat 2013). The vocabularies used in libraries or cultural heritage institutions are usually large and have been developed over the course of decades to serve the goals of storing, finding, and accessing a specific collection of objects. The semantics of thesauri differ from the semantics of ontologies: in a thesaurus, real-world objects are modeled as concepts, and may not be referenced directly. This is the same distinction we identified in Chapter 2, where we argued that a skos:Concept describing 'Mark Twain' does not refer to Mark Twain the person unless the description also contains a foaf:focus property. Therefore, thesaurus-matching methods are different from those used for ontology matching, but both involve text mining algorithms.

On the one hand, various linguistic resources, especially multilingual ones, help to reveal the real semantics under different lexical/syntactic forms or labels in different languages, so that lexical matching could detect potential mappings, such as 'Sprinting' (LCSH) – 'Course de vitesse' (Rameau) – 'Kurzstreckenlauf' (SWD). Recently, multilingual knowledge bases such as DBpedia have also been used as background knowledge for matching concepts from different ontologies. The multilingual links within these knowledge bases play a broker's role in connecting concepts with labels in different languages.

On the other hand, library resource descriptions can be treated as instance data that can be used to calculate the similarity of concepts in terms of practical usage. For example, the Dutch concept 'Glomerulopathie' and the FAST concept 'Kidney glomerulus--Diseases' are used to describe similar sets of books in WorldCat catalog data, which reflects their high similarity or relatedness. Such mappings are difficult to obtain from linguistic resources alone (Isaac et al. 2007). But machine-learning techniques reveal the textual similarity between books (as represented by the text of titles, abstracts, and keywords) and the relatedness of their subjects (Wang, Englebienne, and Schlobach 2008). Given the size of the WorldCat database, text mining algorithms could produce more valuable instance-based mappings that have been proven useful in book re-indexing applications (Wang et al. 2012), even in a multilingual context (Wang et al. 2009). In fact, instance-based matching techniques can be useful to detect mappings which are not strict equivalence links, such as the skos:broadMatch and skos:relatedMatch relations from the SKOS model, which are derived from thesaurus standards.

The matching methods described here, especially instance-based ones, are actually generic enough to be applied to other problems involving entity identification. Anticipating the discussion in the next section, Table 4.1 shows excerpts from descriptions available from WorldCat for the World War II memoir *American Guerrilla*, which a human reader might perceive as redundant. Failure analysis reveals that records that might be collapsed into a single description are maintained as distinct descriptions because some of them cite Brassey's as the publisher, while others cite Potomac Books. But if an instance-based mapping method was applied in this context to reveal that the two publisher names appear in essentially the same contexts, it would be possible to infer, correctly, that these publishers are related because Brassey's is an imprint of Potomac Books. Similarly, if two author name strings are associated with similar publications (in terms of subjects, word usages, co-authors, etc.), it is likely that these two names refer to the same person. Even if the final decisions still need human intervention, finding potentially linked candidates could reduce the problem space enormously.

From a broader perspective, the same method could be used to identify similar entities such as journals. Starting from the simple hypothesis that similar journals publish similar articles, we have measured similarities among 35 thousand journals using metadata associated with 67 million articles that have been published in them (Koopman and Wang 2014). The article metadata, derived primarily from the title and abstract, is aggregated per journal and the similarity is calculated from aggregated text. Treating the WorldCat database as a large corpus, this method has shown the potential to identify similar journals in certain research fields and, more interestingly, 'broker' journals connecting multiple disciplines.

4.3.2   LINKED LIBRARY VOCABULARIES

Once vocabularies are mapped, a user needs to use only one concept label to retrieve all records described by concepts with the same semantics, under either monolingual or multilingual circumstances. For example, when a user searches for books with the subject 'Course de vitesse,' books with the subject of 'Sprinting' or 'Kurzstreckenlauf' should also be returned. This is only possible when concepts from different thesauri are properly linked. As shown in Figure 4.10, via a set of skos:closeMatch properties, this Rameau[2] concept is linked to three SWD[3] concepts, one LCSH concept, and one Dewey code.

When vocabularies and authority files maintained by libraries are represented in a more machine-processable format with machine-understandable semantics, they are ready for wider exposure. Figure 4.11 depicts an example of linked library vocabularies published by the W3C Library Linked Data Incubator Group in 2011 (Isaac et al. 2011). The connections among these vocabularies are generated automatically—in some cases, to datasets outside the Library domain, such as DBpedia and Freebase. When such semantic links have been defined, legacy data curated by libraries can be integrated into the web of data, where it can be leveraged to support the next generation of Semantic Web applications. In return, the work of linguists and lexicographers in the broader community would be available to enrich the Concept entities defined in the library community.

---

2. Rameau (Répertoire d'autorité-matière encyclopédique et alphabétique unifié) maintained by the Bibliothèque nationale de France.
3. SWD (Schlagwortnormdatei) maintained by the Deutsche Nationalbibliothek.

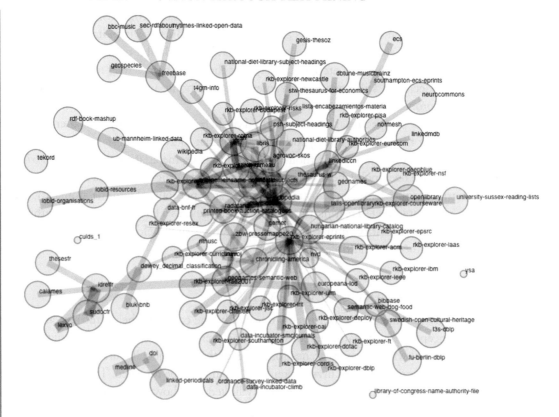

Figure 4.11: Linked library vocabularies (Isaac et al. 2011).

4.4   CLUSTERING

Document clustering is a fundamental task of text mining, through which more efficient organization, navigation, summarization, and retrieval of documents may be achieved. Automatic clustering is especially important for large-scale aggregations containing many records describing similar or related content. If such records are not grouped in some meaningful way, the information seeker is confronted with results that appear to be redundant or messy.

Clusters may reveal duplicate documents or important entities and relationships, such as those defined in the model of creative works discussed in Chapter 3. Of these, duplicates are most visible to the reader, seemingly the most straightforward to address, but the most difficult to resolve. OCLC's installed production processes remove identical records by checking similarities among highly reliable numeric or controlled strings such as the ISBN, author, title, edition statement, and physical description. But the multiple versions of *American Guerrilla* elude this process because the ten descriptions available from WorldCat are all slightly different, as the descriptions in Table 4.1 reveal.[4]

Table 4.1: Different versions of *American Guerrilla* available from WorldCat

Record	Format	Edition	Publisher
1	Book	2005	Washington, D.C. : Potomac Books
2	Book : Biography	2005. 1st Memories of war ed	Washington, D.C. : Brassey's
3	Book : Biography	2005. 1st Memories of war ed	Washington, D.C. : Potomac
4	Book	2005. Soft cover	Washington, D.C. : Potomac Books
5	Book	2003	Dulles, Va. : Potomac Books, Inc.
6	Book : Biography	2003 1st. Memories of war ed	Washington, D.C. : Brassey's
7	Book : Biography	1991	Washington : London : Brassey's (US)
8	Book : Biography	1990	Washington : Brassey's (US)
9	Book : Biography	1990	Washington [u.a.] : Brassey
10	eBook : Document: Biography	1990	Washington : Brassey's (US)

The data shown in Table 4.1 represents a failure, a success, and a set of goals for further research. It can be interpreted as a failure because records 1 and 3 are so similar that a more sophisticated string-matching algorithm might have been able to eliminate one of them as a duplicate. Such a result could be visible in a future version of WorldCat.org because OCLC's duplicate-detection algorithms are constantly being revised. But the data also represents a success because it is the result of the clustering algorithm discussed in Chapter 3, which identifies Manifestations of the same Work. Of course, future versions of the WorldCat.org user interface need to be more explicit about the common characteristics of the Work entity that underlies this list—that it is a memoir published by a survivor of a Japanese internment camp in World War II and is available in the multiple formats shown here. Finally, the descriptions listed in Table 4.1 show the need for more research on the problem of identifying real-world entities and relationships in noisy textual data. For example, the knowledge that Brassey's is an imprint of Potomac Books would make it

---

4. Derived from the results list accessible at: `https://web.archive.org/web/20140915003245/http:` `//www.worldcat.org/title/american-guerilla-my-war-behind-japanese-lines/oclc/232006160/editio` `ns?editionsView=true&referer=br`.

possible to label records 2 and 3 as duplicates because they point to the same object. Moreover, records 9 and 10 have exactly the same content because 10 is a digitized version of 9.

Sorting out these issues is a major task, but clustering algorithms provide a useful start. Chapter 3 showed that clustering algorithms are already being used in many OCLC projects to identify related groups of creative works. But the inputs are restricted to highly reliable structured data, such as names, titles, and subject headings, because the processes must operate fully automatically in a production environment, which has little tolerance for error and places a premium on computational efficiency. As a research project, we are also investigating what can be learned from clustering algorithms that measure similarity on the complete text of a resource description and are evaluated by human judgment with the goal of creating a dignostic tool for knowledge discovery. This work focuses on relationships among Items, providing input to a model and the design of a process that will eventually be able to run without human supervision.

Our analysis has shown that, depending on the data attributes and the (dis)similarity measures used by the clustering algorithm, clusters may reveal the presence of close or exact textual duplicates, identical real-world referents, or real-world referents that are connected to one another in some fashion. From a broader semantic perspective, digital objects could be connected based on many different dimensions, forming clusters around similar periods of time, geo-locations, subjects, people, events, etc. For example, Figure 4.12 depicts a group of images that could be grouped together by different criteria—as pictures of the same real-world person, as objects curated in the same collections, or as people with the same job title. Other use cases might require the exploration of a cluster that contains pictures of the people who share the same office or go to the same school. Once exposed as linked data, these clusters of different granularities could enable users to explore large-scale aggregations in a much more flexible and exploratory way.

This result was demonstrated in our experiment of clustering on an aggregated collection of metadata about cultural heritage materials (Wang et al. 2013). Collaborating with a development team responsible for the publication of Europeana, we were interested in identifying related Cultural Heritage objects (CHOs) at different levels of similarity, which potentially reflect different semantic relations among them. As depicted in Figure 4.13, we provided clusters at five similarity levels, with level 100 giving near-duplicates and level 20 the most vaguely connected objects. A user could thus explore the collections to find CHOs with different levels of relatedness. A more detailed study reveals the typology of groupings, which cover a broad range of relations defined in the Europeana Data Model (Europeana 2014), such as same objects/duplicate records, views of the same object, parts of an object, derivative works, collections, and thematic groupings. This finding is a good match with the multi-dimensionality of CHOs, even if the similarity used in the clustering is purely based on textual data. However, this approach could not benefit from the semantic information embedded in the data itself. For example, if we treat the content of the dc:creator field as person name string instead of simple text, we could calculate the similarity of CHOs based on their creators. The same goes for many other metadata fields, such as dc:subject, dc:publisher, etc. For the free-text fields, such as dc:title and dc:description, a good information ex-

Eyre, James
(Austrian National Library)

Sir **James Eyre** (1734-1799),
Chief Justice of the Common Pleas
(Government Art Collection)

Sir John Eardley Wilmot (1709-1792)
Chief Justice of the Common Pleas
(Government Art Collection)

Figure 4.12: Multidimensional similarities.

traction process needs to be applied first to extract valuable semantic information based on which the clustering process could produce more sensible semantic clusters along different dimensions.

In the future, large-scale digital libraries will host more and more heterogeneous digital objects. For example, tens of millions of digital objects are already automatically ingested into WorldCat through the Digital Collection Gateway (OCLC 2014e). Thus it is important to apply clustering algorithms and other semantic technologies to discover meaningful relationships among digital objects that can populate richer data models. These efforts are mutually reinforcing and a subject of emerging work at OCLC, which we will mention briefly in Chapter 5.

4.5   CHAPTER SUMMARY

This chapter has surveyed some of the most promising text mining algorithms that are already being used to promote text to machine-processable data in library resource descriptions. These

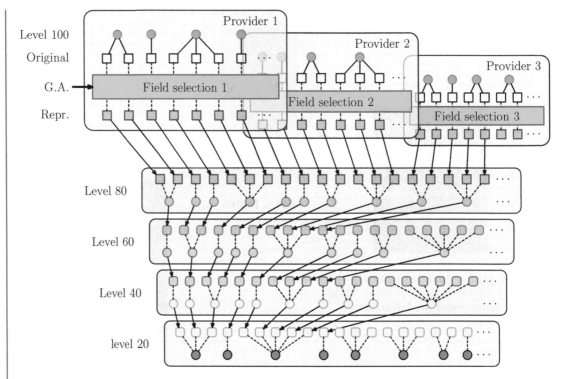

Figure 4.13: Hierarchical structuring of CHOs at different similarity levels (Wang et al. 2013).

results are valuable in their own right, but they also have cascading effects that feed into the process flow for generating the empirical evidence for OCLC's linked data models. Cleaner descriptions of creative works improve the performance of the Works cluster algorithms described in Chapter 3. Evidence gathered along the way can also be applied to the improvement of authoritative hubs for other entities that are mentioned in bibliographic data maintained by libraries. In sum, what we have described here is part of the pipeline for iterative improvement of OCLC's bibliographic and authority data; or more precisely in the linked data architecture, the repositories for authoritative information about the entities required for library resource descriptions that are earmarked for publication on the broader Web. Text mining algorithms are a key component and will become more and more important as these resources continue to grow.

CHAPTER 5

The Library Linked Data Cloud

5.1   A LOOK BACK AND FORWARD

The projects described in the previous pages highlight the importance of entities and relationships in library data, which are already expressed in legacy standards, but are now recaptured in a format that is more capable of broadcasting the value of library collections to the broader Web. Focusing on the identification of six key entities—Person, Place, Organization, Concept, Work, and Object—the exposition describes the process of designing Linked Data models and discovering evidence for them through the retrospective conversion of library authority and bibliographic records.

Some might object that the scope of the projects has been too narrow because our models describe only monographs, not digital or multimedia resources; and because the exposition has focused on the publication of linked data, not its consumption. Our attention has been restricted to the publication of identifiers that fall squarely within the scope of traditional librarianship—for creative works, not raw data, and for book authors, not unpublished researchers or agents in a collection of historical documents. But work we have described is a baseline that establishes continuity with the past. It shows where library linked data models have come from and how they can be populated. It makes the case that these models can become a core component of the architecture for the next generation of library resource description. Our goal in writing this book is to establish common ground for discussion with librarians, standards experts, and computer scientists beyond OCLC and to serve as a springboard for more sophisticated work.

5.2   NEXT STEPS

We have argued that the development of models for library resource description can be grounded in Schema.org—not only because it is the most widely adopted vocabulary for exposing structured data on the Web and is recognized by the world's major search engines—but for the far simpler reason that it is a sophisticated standard first published during a time of historic instability in the evolution of standards for library resource description. In our first experiments with Schema.org in 2011, we created descriptions of creative works, reformulating bibliographic records as graphs, but we have recently republished the RDF models for FAST and VIAF with references to schema:Person, schema:Organization, schema:Place, and schema:CreativeWork—the top-level concepts described in library authority files and aggregations of them.

We believe that the case for using Schema.org is compelling, despite our own initial reservations and those that continue to be expressed by colleagues and peers in the library community who are solving similar problems. But what happens to the models we have developed if the most important search engines stop supporting Schema.org? Right now, such a move seems unlikely, given the utility of structured data for search engines and the fact that Schema.org is the first Semantic Web standard to have gained widespread acceptance and the rate of adoption is increasing (Guha 2014). The survival of Schema.org is not guaranteed, of course, at least not in the timeframe presupposed in the traditional practice of librarianship. The MARC standard was first published over fifty years ago; will Schema.org persist into the 2060s? Even if it does not, Schema.org has already served as a vehicle for consolidating the best ideas about knowledge engineering on a large scale, starting from its roots in Cyc in the early 1980s and continuing with the innovations introduced by its growing user community, including the Schema Bib Extend group managed by OCLC's Richard Wallis. Through engagement with Schema.org and the Semantic Web principles it represents, we have become accustomed to the discipline of modeling the things in the world that users care the most about. If that goal is achieved, it is the best insurance against future disruption because such models can be more easily mapped to whatever ontology takes Schema.org's place.

In fact, some leaders are already making the much stronger case that it is not only possible to align the descriptive standards preferred by librarians with those adopted in the broader Web, but that it is necessary and even more important than a continued investment in library-community standards. For example, Kenning Arlitsch, Dean of the Library at Montana State University, argues that recent attempts to modernize library standards have been met with mixed results, concluding that:

> "If we believe there's value to making our materials discoverable and usable to a wider audience of people, then we must begin a concerted effort to make our metadata interoperable with Web standards and to publish to platforms that more people use. Well-intentioned librarians and archivists have spent decades developing and implementing data interchange formats that simply haven't been adopted by the Internet, and as a result we struggle to make our materials visible and usable. Is it appropriate, or even responsible, for us to continue to push an environment where people aren't, or where they don't even seem to want to be?" (Arlitsch 2014), p. 619

Another set of concerns stems from observations about the scope and shape of Schema.org. If it is an ontology designed primarily for describing products and services traded in the commercial sector, how can it be detailed enough to describe library resources with the care required for long-term stewardship? We believe that this question can be answered by a ground-up approach: developing models derived from Schema.org, testing them on real instance data produced by the library community, and improving them with input from domain experts. That is how the models described in this book were developed and they are only the foundation for what we believe is possible.

For example, digital copies of scholarly articles and monographs present one opportunity to explore as-yet unused properties defined by Schema.org and address a pressing need for improved library resource description. Figure 5.1 shows the relationship between a hardcopy monograph and a PDF version, using the property schema:encodesCreativeWork. Since a PDF representation may consist either of a single large file or a set of separate files containing chapters, pages, or other logical components, it can be modeled as a hierarchical collection with schema:isPartOf relationships to the parent.

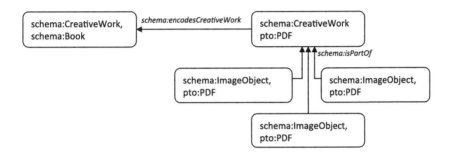

Figure 5.1: Relationships between print and digital copies of the same Work.

With this model, it is possible to state that the two versions have the same author, title, subject, and exactly the same text. But in a university library, the two versions would probably have different terms of access: the monograph might circulate to library-card holders for a limited time period, while the PDF file could be accessed for any length of time with or without authentication as a member of the local community. In the language of the Holdings model described in Chapter 3, the PDF and hardcopy versions are creative works realized as different kinds of schema:Product, for which different terms of accessibility can be specified in a schema:Offer description.

These relationships are used for a different purpose in Figure 5.2, a slight elaboration of the model depicted in Figure 5.1, which depicts a high-level model of a journal article, expressed in recently published vocabulary defined by Schema.org. At the center is schema:Article, which has a schema:isPartOf relationship to a journal issue, coded as schema:Issue. An 'Issue' is a subdivision of 'Periodical,' coded as schema:Periodical, which has a schema:ISSN property. Not shown is an analogous relationship to schema:PublicationVolume. As in Figure 5.1, the contents of a journal article can be realized either as a physical document or a digital file. Since the ISSN is a product model analogous to an ISBN, the journal article, volume, issue, and periodical have a physical presence, which would trigger the assignment of a value from the schema:Product class and permit the statement of a schema:Offer in the OCLC model of Works. The diagram shows that a printed journal article is available from Montana State University and a digital surrogate is accessible from EBSCO (2015).

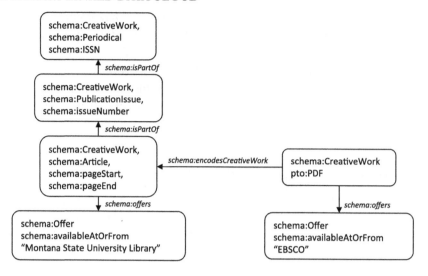

Figure 5.2: Relationships between print and digital copies of the same Work.

The model shown in Figure 5.2 is only a draft and many details still need to be specified, but it builds on previous work and shows a new area of interest for linked data models at OCLC. It is an extension of the OCLC Model of Works described in Chapter 3 and is expressed almost entirely in Schema.org. It also permits the expression of subtle relationships in a machine-processable format that are coded only as free text in current standards. For example, Figure 5.2 reveals that models of holdings are fundamentally different for physical and print resources: a library holds—or 'has'—a physical object that can be put into the hands of a patron, while the same library does not own but merely licenses a digital surrogate from a commercial provider.

Finally, the model illustrates the workflow we have developed in the past year. The first draft of the model is defined using Schema.org and gaps are identified. In this example, 'PDF' is represented in the pto: namespace because it is not yet defined either in Schema.org or BiblioGraph. But a serviceable definition is available in the Product Types Ontology (PTO 2015), which is the output of a software process that converts concepts defined in Wikipedia to a machine-understandable format and models them as subclasses of schema:Product. When the model matures and the definition of 'PDF' needs to be upgraded, we can define it in BiblioGraph with input from other experts in bibliographic description. But since a good definition of 'PDF' is likely to be needed by other communities besides librarians and publishers, this term is a candidate for inclusion in Schema.org. Using BiblioGraph.net, we can pinpoint the location of 'PDF' in the larger ontology, making minor adjustments where necessary and lobbying the managers of Schema.org to do the same. The structured parts of the journal article were defined in a similar fashion by the Schema Bib Extend Community Group and were formally absorbed into Schema.org in September 2014 (Wallis and Cohen 2014), (Wallis 2014a). Though additional effort will be required to define vocabulary that expresses some of the fine details in the accessibility contracts as properties of schema:Offer, the procedure for doing so is already in place. This project is far from mature, but Mixter, OBrien, and Arlitsch Mixter, OBrien, and Arlitsch (2014) describe a project using the same workflow that has already produced a working model of theses and dissertations in the context of a university institutional repository.

We are often asked if the linked data models OCLC has developed are detailed enough to replace MARC as the standard for data storage and communication between libraries. It is too early to know. Other library-community initiatives, most notably BIBFRAME and RDA, have been addressing use cases for the long-term management of library resources and the sharing of data among libraries.

A possible alignment of these standards with the OCLC model of Works is shown in Figure 5.3; it sketches the same landscape as Figure 4.1 in Godby (2013) from a slightly broader perspective. At the core is a detailed description that supports library functions described in a native library standard. The elements of the description that are comprehensible and relevant to the broader Web are mapped to Schema.org and candidates for proposed Schema extensions defined in BiblioGraph. Since only a small number of the concepts in the domain of library resource description can be exposed in an easy-to-use vocabulary that serves the needs of the entire Semantic Web, the analysis required to optimize the exposure of our resources is no different from that being conducted by other user communities, such as medicine, sports, the automotive industry, and others mentioned in Guha (2014). Nevertheless, if the library standards community succeeds in engaging with the managers of Schema.org, the mapping from native standards will be achieved with minimal loss of information.

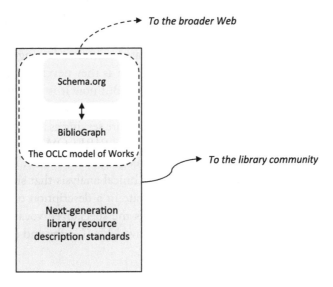

Figure 5.3: The OCLC model of Works aligned with library resource description standards.

Some have asked the arguably less important question about the relative size of the two main areas in the diagram. The short answer is that it shouldn't matter because the description that can be exposed to the broader Web should be a proper subset of the description required for internal library processes. Libraries benefit if that subset is as large as possible, but we don't know whether the subset is large or small. Perhaps it is relatively large because it may be possible to say more with modern standards that encode entity-relationship models and have a built-in vocabulary for describing resource types that didn't exist when MARC was first defined. But a more nuanced answer recognizes that the task of resource description will change in the new environment. For example, the development of authoritative hubs implies an expanded role for authority control and a diminished role for original description, but the hubs themselves require maintenance that will be absorbed into a human-guided workflow. As we pointed out in Chapters 3 and 4, the assignment of URIs is most reliable when the source is an authority record or a controlled access field in a MARC record, both created from human expertise; other sources require text-mining algorithms that also require human input, usually in the form of training data. When the description of library resources is more broadly integrated into the Semantic Web, however, some tasks may no longer be necessary. For example, copy cataloging would become obsolete in a data infrastructure featuring persistent URIs for Works and Manifestations. Instead of making a copy of a record, librarians would create a statement that includes one of these URIs, supplementing it with local detail required to describe an individual item and its availability. In addition, descriptions of resources originating from the publisher supply chain would be usable in their native forms if publishers produced bibliographic descriptions modeled in Schema.org instead of ONIX, with which it is compatible.

As we have pointed out, the OCLC projects began to take shape at the same time as experiments and standards initiatives in the library community with other primary goals, producing models with comparable granularity. But maturation required a period of introspection, as we developed resource entity hubs and a more sophisticated workflow for engaging with Schema.org. The sponsors of BIBFRAME and RDA did the same as they developed vocabulary and refined the details of their models (LC 2014b; DNB 2014). But now it is time to join forces again because the path forward looks unclear to those who must build out the new standards for library resource description. Accordingly, OCLC researchers are serving as advisors on two grant-funded projects, Linked Data for Libraries (LD4L 2015b) and BIBFLOW (BF 2015), whose goal is to produce BIBFRAME descriptions in a library cataloging environment. In addition, OCLC and the Library of Congress are collaborating on a technical analysis that shows how BIBFRAME and the OCLC model of Works would interoperate in a description of a library resource that cannot be described easily in MARC and requires the specialized vocabulary developed in the library community. A high-level summary is now available (Godby and Denenberg 2015).

5.3 A FEW LESSONS AND SOME PERSISTENT CHALLENGES

The projects described in the previous section will be developed through the familiar cycle of analysis, design, implementation, public release, and iterative improvement, following the same process that produced the results described in earlier chapters. We have learned many lessons, all starting from the realization that though the linked data paradigm is rooted in good ideas of the past, it is radical, unsettling, and still experimental. Thus it should not be surprising that linked data meets resistance among targeted users as well as colleagues who are tasked with its implementation. To increase the comfort level, we participate in community standards initiatives and public conversation. We communicate the linked data vision, highlighting the successes of others when it is not quite visible in our work. We provide many pathways to understanding, including publications, presentations, workshops, collaborative projects, published datasets, demonstrations of our technology stack, and even one-on-one tutorials. To address more narrow technical concerns at OCLC, we listen to colleagues who are trying to consume the data we are publishing. We discourage prolonged investment in solutions that mix old and new paradigms because they are backward-looking and difficult to maintain. Instead, we recommend investment in more robust prototypes, which are developed in accordance with the lifecycle requirements that govern traditional products and services. Whenever a roadmap for a linked data resource delivers a feature in time for a product to make use of it, we gain an ally.

To get this far, we have also confronted many challenges, but some are persistent and perhaps endemic to the enterprise of publishing linked data for public consumption.

5.3.1 CONCEPTUAL CHALLENGES

Despite the apparent complexity of the linked data paradigm, as documented in a growing collection of standards documents from multiple communities of practice, only some of which were discussed in Chapter 1, producing linked data reduces to three straightforward tasks. The first is the development of a model of real-world entities and relationships for a domain of interest. The second task is the production of instance data, or an RDF dataset, which mentions these entities and provides more information about them that could be mined by a subsequent process. Finally, the authoritative documents that define the entities must be associated with a persistent identifier, or URI, which is embedded in the documents that mention them. References to the real-world objects beyond the documents is established when the URI is resolved with currently available Web protocols. We have argued throughout this book that librarians are already familiar with these tasks. The linked data paradigm is simply a set of conventions that promises greater interoperability and persistence for the outcomes that their work already generates.

But model design is difficult. Though an obvious starting point is the collection of prior successes, we have learned that even the models of ontologically simple objects must be assembled from multiple sources and will probably be works in progress for the foreseeable future. For example, we argued in Chapter 2 that the model of 'Person' encoded in a library authority file describes a unique individual who is attested either as an author or a subject in the published record. The simplest acceptable machine-processable model of 'Person' for the domain of librarianship requires one or more names, a unique identifier, a set of properties that identify lifespan dates, a connection between the Person and the Work, and more fundamentally, a connection between the Person and the modeled description. But no single published model of the 'Person' entity contains all of these properties and the most recent model of VIAF had to be derived from library authority files and supplemented with classes and properties defined in multiple Semantic Web standards, such as schema:Person, foaf:focus, and skos:Concept.

In addition, the growth of VIAF and other entity hubs for Persons will exert pressure for even more properties that describe affiliations for professional researchers and define a larger set of roles of creators and contributors in the production of raw research outputs and multimedia objects, which may not be formally published but disseminated through other channels. The result will be an improvement over current descriptive practice, but it will be obtained through a process of continual refinement as new use cases are considered. As we pointed out at the end of Chapter 2, the same process will undoubtedly guide the creation of a linked data model of the 'Place' and 'Organization' entities, though current clues indicate that these models may well come from outside the library community, as will the resource hubs themselves. For example, Smith-Yoshimura et al. (2014) reports that major universities are already building authoritative hubs that describe their own researchers, though they are not necessarily modeled as linked data. Even so, this new landscape is an improvement over current library descriptive practice and a validation of the linked data paradigm, which promotes the value of sharing the burden of description of the real-world objects that are important to multiple communities.

Regardless of how these entities are modeled, the assignment of identifiers to individual people, places, and organizations is conceptually straightforward. But the same cannot be said of concepts or topics, the other category of entities described in library authority files. For example, O'Neill (2014) observed that only 5.8 percent of the Library of Congress subject headings that appear in bibliographic descriptions in WorldCat are said to be established and have corresponding LCSH authority records; as of January, 2014, 24.8 million headings do not. From a linked data perspective, this result implies that no resolvable URI can be assigned to nearly 94% of the LCSH headings accessible from the WorldCat cataloging data because they do not have unique identifiers or authoritative descriptions. This analysis also reveals that most of the unauthorized headings are topical subjects. They are an expected consequence of the LCSH design, which has been labeled 'synthetic' by classification experts because it features a small set of editorially maintained terms and a rich set of production rules applied by catalogers to create unique headings that describe the object in hand.

To be more precise, the O'Neill statistics overestimate the size of the problem with the LCSH topical headings because some of the unauthorized terms reflect the natural rate of vocabulary growth that can be managed in an editorial process—as more people, places, and organizations appear in the published record and cultural change produces new things to talk and write about. As we pointed out in Chapter 2, complex headings built from established terms can also be assigned multiple identifiers, such as 'Burns and scalds—patients,' whose meaning can be interpreted as the union of 'Burns and scalds,' with a URI containing the identifier 'sh85018164' and 'Patients,' with a URI containing the identifier 'sh00006930.'

But a generic solution is elusive because of what linguists would recognize as a fundamental difference between a vocabulary and a grammar: the terms in a vocabulary can be counted, but the outputs of a grammar with productive, or recursive, rules cannot. Thus it is impossible to assign identifiers to all of the sentences in English or Chinese because they form an infinite set, which can expand whenever a speaker or writer says something. But even if such assignments could be made, it would be an absurd task to identify the sentences that are worthy of curation and associate those expressing the same or related thoughts. This is an upper limit in the creation of linked data from natural language.

On a smaller scale, this is the problem exhibited by library authority files with a synthetic design. The number of catalogers producing unique headings as part of their normal workflow is far greater than the number of editors who can upgrade the authority files that have been affected by their work. We agree with O'Neill that the upper limit can be sidestepped by populating authoritative linked data hubs with subject headings built with an enumerative, not a synthetic design, which feature a larger vocabulary and a minimal set of production rules. We argued in Chapter 2 that FAST is one such scheme; and it is a subset of LCSH, in which every term is established. In Chapter 1, we pointed out that FAST headings have been algorithmically applied to the experimental version of WorldCat from which the RDFa markup is published, using the publicly accessible LCSH-to-FAST conversion program (OCLC 2011a). Thus we can assign URIs to many of the cataloger-supplied topical subject headings accessible from the WorldCat cataloging data through an alternative route.

5.3.2 TECHNICAL CHALLENGES

The technical goal of the projects reported in this book is to develop full-sized implementations, not small prototypes. At the outset, we were unsure if it was possible to build the RDF datasets of the required size with real-time access. But as of August 2014, we can report the following statistics from datastores that can be queried from reasonably responsive interfaces: 300 million RDF triples in the Dewey Decimal Classification; 2 billion triples in VIAF; 5 billion triples in WorldCat Works; 15 billion triples in the WorldCat Catalog; and approximately 5 trillion triples in a larger corpus accessible from WorldCat.org that includes descriptions of e-journal articles.

In short, our tests have demonstrated that we can work at the scale required to address the most important problems in the domain of library resource description with a technology stack that consists primarily of open source utilities. In more human-centered terms, OCLC has put together a workflow that automates the conversion from legacy standards, facilitates data analysis and model development, and creates RDF outputs that are capable of standing alone and can coexist with legacy systems. Our development environment is designed to engage collaborators with diverse skill sets, including subject-matter and modeling experts who are not professional programmers as well as software engineers with industry-standard backgrounds in SQL database design, XML processing, and Java development. The details of our technical environment have to be deferred to a separate communication, but a summary is offered in Mixter, OBrien, and Arlitsch (2014).

The primary output of the OCLC linked data implementation is a large network of data that conforms to an entity-relationship model of library resources, in which machine-processable statements can be made that were not possible in the legacy standards. These statements can be understood across multiple data stores inside OCLC or elsewhere in the library community and can be consumed by third parties without the need for dedicated 'reader' software. This is a major technical achievement because it is a proof of concept for the infrastructure that can broadcast the value of library collections to the broader Web, where users are most likely to begin their quest for information.

But given our primary use case and our endorsement of Schema.org, the ontology recognized by the world's most prominent search engines, we are seeking an even bigger reward: greater visibility for libraries on the Web through syndication. But right now, 'visibility on the Web' has multiple interpretations. To some, it is appropriate structured data returned from a Google search, such as the before-and-after screenshots of the Google Knowledge Card for the Montana State University Library, whose vital facts appeared in the correct form only after the authors had submitted an article about their institution to Wikipedia (Arlitsch et al. 2014). To others, visibility is measured in increased clickthroughs from external sources; and to others, it is the appearance of their structured data in Google's Webmaster tools. These are tantalizing hints that data has arrived at its intended destination, but questions remain about how it is processed by search engines and how much the Schema.org markup matters. To answer such questions, we must acquire a deeper understanding of the linked data cloud. During the next three years, we will collaborate with the Arlitsch team, who are experts in search engine optimization for library resources (Arlitsch and OBrien 2013). With financial support from a grant awarded to Montana State University by the Institute of Museum and Library Studies in September 2014, we are developing and testing models to increase the Web visibility of university-managed institutional repositories, documenting the steps required for achieving success.

5.3.3   ENVIRONMENTAL CHALLENGES

This book has described OCLC's effort to publish linked data on the Web. But how do OCLC's projects and others published by the library community contribute to the Semantic Web? To find out, Smith-Yoshimura (2014a) conducted an online survey of publishers and consumers of linked data in the library community. The survey elicited 72 respondents, 51 of whom are linked data publishers; nearly every project discussed in this book is represented, plus many others. In decreasing order of RDF triple count, the largest datasets being consumed by the survey participants are WorldCat, WorldCat Works, Europeana, and The European Library (TEL 2014b), a

Web portal that provides access to the collections of 48 national and research libraries in Europe. The most commonly used data standards for publication are those discussed in this book: SKOS, FOAF, Dublin Core, Dublin Core Terms, and Schema.org. The pattern of linked data consumption among the survey participants is summarized in Table 5.1. Third-party datasets consumed by OCLC's linked data projects are highlighted in red. The tabulated survey responses are also represented as a bar graph in Figure 5.4.

Table 5.1: Library linked data consumption patterns. Adapted from (Smith-Yoshimura 2014a)

Datasets consumed by survey participants	Count of participants consuming
DBpedia, GeoNames, id.loc.gov, VIAF	20 or more
FAST, WorldCat, Art and Architecture Thesaurus (Getty)	10-19
Wikidata, WorldCat Works, The European Library, ORCID, ISNI, Dewey Decimal Classification, Digital Public Library of America, Europeana, British National Bibliography, Canadian Subject Headings	1-9

The datasets mentioned in Table 5.1 and Figure 5.4 were listed in the survey questions, but participants were also invited to supply the names of other resources they are consuming. The long list of responses includes http://data.bnf.fr from the Bibliothèque nationale de France (BNF 2014), the Linked Data Service from the Deutsche Nationalbibliothek (DNB 2015), and the General Multilingual Environmental Thesaurus (GMET 2014). A spreadsheet containing the complete set of raw responses is also Web-accessible (OCLC 2014c).

Since the survey results became available just as this book was going to production, they capture the same moment in time, complementing the insider's perspective documented in the previous pages with a glimpse of the broader landscape. The survey is not a scientific sample, and we have to interpret the results with caution, but it sparks impressions that can be validated by other lines of inquiry. For example, the interest in linked data by the library community is international. The cloud is still organizing itself, but it is centered on http://id.loc.gov and VIAF, the oldest datasets published by the library community. DBpedia and GeoNames also figure prominently, anchoring library linked data to the center of the iconic Linked Open Data cloud for the broader Web (Cyganiac and Jensch 2014), mentioned in the opening pages of Chapter 1. Many cutting-edge projects are still emerging—such as WorldCat Works; services that assign persistent identifiers to researchers, such as ISNI (ISNI 2014) and ORCID (ORCID 2015); and the Digital Public Library of America (DPLA 2014), the first national digital library of the United States, whose contents are freely accessible. Even more nascent are the linked data resources named by the survey participants, many of which were not published by libraries but by organizations that serve individual areas of study. When this survey is repeated later in 2015,

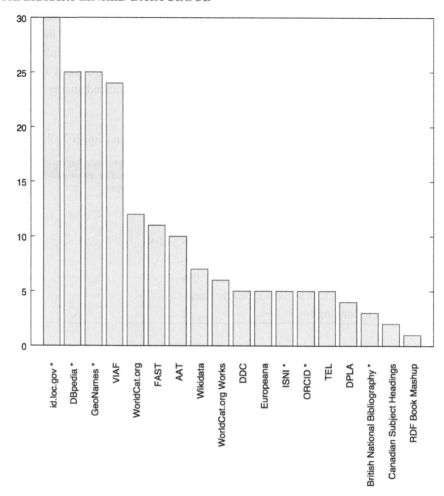

Figure 5.4: Library linked data consumption: a tabulation. Adapted from Smith-Yoshimura (2014a).

we expect the landscape to be more populated and interconnected, replicating the trajectory of change observed in the LOD cloud diagram.

The survey also sheds light on the impact of OCLC's linked data projects, whose datasets are among the oldest, largest, and most widely consumed. But a future imperative for OCLC is to create more connections among the resources published by libraries and affiliated communities, starting with the initiatives described in this chapter. As members of an international community, we share the same aspirations: to demonstrate that library resource descriptions can be promoted from the web of documents to the Web of Data, and to use the new architecture to broaden the reach of libraries. If we succeed, we will have realized the vision of integrating libraries with the broader Web, where they can connect to users in their native environment and deliver the resources they request at no cost. This act of fulfillment is a reminder that the public mission of libraries can be advanced through a better integration with the commercial interests that populate the Semantic Web. But the service offered by libraries is unique.

Bibliography

Arlitsch, Kenning. 2014. "Being Irrelevant: How Library Data Interchange Standards Have Kept Us Off the Internet." *Journal of Library Administration* 54 (7): 609–619. doi:10.1080/01930826.2014.964031.

Arlitsch, Kenning, and Patrick OBrien, eds. 2013. *Improving the Visibility and Use of Digital Repositories through SEO: A LITA Guide.* Chicago, Illinois, USA: American Library Association.

Arlitsch, Kenning, Patrick OBrien, Jason A. Clark, Scott W. H. Young, and Doralyn Rossmann. 2014. "Demonstrating Library Value at Network Scale: Leveraging the Semantic Web with New Knowledge Work." *Journal of Library Administration* 54 (5): 413–425. http://www.tandfonline.com/doi/pdf/10.1080/01930826.2014.946778.

Baker, Thomas, Emmanuelle Bermès, Karen Coyle, Gordon Dunsire, Antoine Isaac, Peter Murray, Michael Panzer, et al. 2011. "Library Linked Data Incubator Final Report." W3C Incubator Group Report, 25 October. World Wide Web Consortium. http://www.w3.org/2005/Incubator/lld/XGR-lld-20111025/.

Beckett, David, and Tim Berners-Lee. 2011. "Turtle: Terse RDF Triple Language." W3C Team Submission, 28 March. World Wide Web Consortium. http://www.w3.org/TeamSubmission/turtle/.

Bell, Graham. 2012. "ONIX for E-Books." In *Part 2: Find That E-book – Or Not: How Metadata Matters. Understanding Critical Elements of E-books: Standards for Formatting and Metadata.* NISO Webinar, 21 March. http://www.niso.org/news/events/2012/nisowebinars/ebooks_metadata/.

Bennett, Rick, Brian F. Lavoie, and Edward T. O'Neill. 2002. "The Concept of a Work in WorldCat: An Application of FRBR." *Library Collections, Acquisitions, and Technical Services* 27 (1): 45–59. doi:10.1016/S1464-9055(02)00306-8.

Berners-Lee, Tim. 2001. "Issue 14: What is the Range of the HTTP Dereference Function?" *Technical Architecture Group Issue Tracking*, 25 March. World Wide Web Consortium. http://www.w3.org/2001/tag/group/track/issues/14.

———. 2006. "Linked Data." In *Design Issues: Architectural and Philosophical Points*, 27 July. World Wide Web Consortium. http://www.w3.org/DesignIssues/LinkedData.html.

Berners-Lee, Tim. 2007. "Giant Global Graph." In *timbl's blog*, 21 November. http://dig.csail.mit.edu/breadcrumbs/node/215.

Berners-Lee, Tim, James Hendler, and Ora Lasilla. 2001. "The Semantic Web: A New Form of Web Content that is Meaningful to Computers Will Unleash a Revolution of New Possibilities." *Scientific American* 284 (5): 28–37.

BF. 2015. "BIBFLOW: An IMLS Project of the UC Davis Library and Zepheira." http://www.lib.ucdavis.edu/bibflow/about/.

BGN. 2014a. "BiblioGraph." BiblioGraph.net. http://bibliograph.net.

———. 2014b. "BiblioGraph.net Core Schema." BiblioGraph.net. http://bibliograph.net/docs/bibliograph_net_rdfa.html.

BL. 2014. "Collection Metadata: Data Services." West Yorkshire, United Kingdom: The British Library. http://www.bl.uk/bibliographic/datafree.html.

BNF. 2014. "About data.bnf.fr." Bibliothèque nationale de France. Last modified 26 November. http://data.bnf.fr.

Brickley, Dan. 2010. "Easier in RDFa: Multiple Types and the Influence of Syntax on Semantics." In *danbr* [blog], 2 November. http://danbri.org/words/2010/11/02/572.

Brickley, Dan, and R.V. Guha. 2004. "RDF Vocabulary Description Language 1.0: RDF Schema." W3C Recommendation, 10 February. World Wide Web Consortium. http://www.w3.org/TR/2004/REC-rdf-schema-20040210/.

———. 2014. "RDF Schema 1.1." W3C Recommendation, 25 February. World Wide Web Consortium. http://www.w3.org/TR/rdf-schema/.

Brickley, Dan, R.V. Guha, and Andrew Layman. 1998. "Resource Description Framework (RDF Schemas)." W3C Working Draft, 9 April. World Wide Web Consortium. http://www.w3.org/TR/1998/WD-rdf-schema-19980409/.

Brickley, Dan, and Libby Miller. 2014. "FOAF Vocabulary Specification 0.99." Namespace Document – Paddington Edition, 14 January. http://xmlns.com/foaf/spec/.

Chan, Lois Mai, and Edward T. O'Neill. 2010. *FAST: Faceted Application of Subject Terminology : Principles and Applications.* Santa Barbara, California, USA: Libraries Unlimited.

CIA. 2015. "The World Factbook." The Central Intelligence Agency. Last modified 5 March. https://www.cia.gov/library/publications/the-world-factbook/.

Connaway, Lynn Silipigni, and Timothy J. Dickey. 2011. "Publisher Names in Bibliographic Data: An Experimental Authority File and a Prototype Application." *Library Resources and Technical Services* 55 (4): 182–194.

Coyle, Karen. 2012. "Taking Library Data From Here to There." NISO/DCMI Webinar, 22 Februray. `http://www.niso.org/apps/group_public/download.php/8071/NISO_DCMIwebinar22february2012PRINT.pdf`.

Cyganiac, Richard, and Anja Jensch. 2014. "Linked Datasets as of August 2014." LOD-Cloud.net. `http://lod-cloud.net/versions/2014-08-30/lod-cloud.svg`.

Dataversity. 2013. "Where Schema.org is At: A Chat With Google's R.V. Guha." In *Dataversity* [blog], 13 November. `http://semanticweb.com/schema-org-chat-googles-r-v-guha_b40607`.

Dawson, Laura. 2012. "Metadata: Without You I'm Nothing (Metadata Quality and its Importance in E-Book Discovery)." In *Part 1: Find That E-Book – Or Not: How Metadata Matters, Understanding Critical Elements of E-books: Standards for Formatting and Metadata*. NISO Webinar, 21 March. `http://www.niso.org/news/events/2012/nisowebinars/ebooks_metadata/`.

DBpedia. 2015. "The DBpedia Knowledge Base." University of Mannheim and Universitaet Leipzig. Last modified 8 January. `http://dbpedia.org/About`.

DCMI. 2007. "DCMI Abstract Model." Dublin Core Metadata Initiative. Last modified 4 June. `http://dublincore.org/documents/abstract-model/`.

DDC. 2014. "Dewey Decimal Classification / Linked Data." OCLC. `http://dewey.info`.

de Melo, Gerard. 2014. "Lexvo.org Main Page." Lexvo.org. `http://www.lexvo.org/`.

de Rosa, Cathy, Joanne Cantrell, Matthew Carlson, Peggy Gallagher, Janet Hawk, and Charlotte Sturtz. 2010. "Perceptions of Libraries: Context and Community." A Report to the OCLC Membership. `http://www.oclc.org/content/dam/oclc/reports/2010perceptions/2010perceptions_all.pdf`.

Dean, Mike, Dan Connolly, Erik van Harmelen, James Hendler, Ian Horrocks, Deborah L. McGuinness, Peter F. Patel-Schneider, and Lynn Andrea Stein, eds. 2002. "OWL 2 Web Ontology Language 1.0 Reference." W3C Working Draft, 29 July. World Wide Web Consortium. `http://www.w3.org/TR/2002/WD-owl-ref-20020729/`.

Dean, Mike, and Guus Schreiber. 2004. "OWL Web Ontology Language Reference." W3C Recommendation, 10 February. World Wide Web Consortium. `http://www.w3.org/TR/owl-ref/`.

Dempsey, Lorcan, Eric Childress, Carol Jean Godby, Thomas B. Hickey, Andrew Houghton, Diane Vizine-Goetz, and Jeff Young. 2005. "Metadata Switch: Thinking about Some Metadata Management and Knowledge Organization Issues in the Changing Research and Learning Landscape." In *Escholarship: A LITA Guide,* edited by Debra Shapiro, 55–79. Chicago, Illinois, USA: LITA Publications.

DNB. 2014. "IFLA Satellite Meeting: RDA Status and Perspectives." Deutsche Nationalbibliotek, Franfurt am Main, Germany, 13 August. `http://www.dnb.de/EN/ Standardisierung/International/iflaSatelliteMeetingProgramm.html`.

———. 2015. "Linked Data Service of the German National Library." Deutsche Nationalbibliothek. Last modified 6 February. `http://www.dnb.de/EN/Service/DigitaleDienste/ LinkedData/linkeddata_node.html`.

Dong, Xin Luna, Evgeniy Gabrilovich, Geremy Heits, Wilko Horn, Ni Lao, Kevin Murphy, Shaohua Sun Thomas Strohmann, and Wei Zhang. 2014. "Knowledge Vault: A Web-Scale Approach to Probabilistic Knowledge Fusion." In *Proceedings of the 20th ACM SIGKDD International Conference on Knowledge Discovery and Data Mining.* New York, New York, USA. Association of Computing Machinery. `https://www.cs.cmu.edu/~nlao/ publication/2014.kdd.pdf`.

DPLA. 2014. "Digital Public Library of America." `http://dp.la`.

Dunsire, Gordon, Diane Hillmann, Jon Phipps, and Karen Coyle. 2011. "A Reconsideration of Mapping in a Semantic World." In *DC-2011: Proceedings of the International Conference on Dublin Core and Metadata Applications.* The Hague, The Netherlands. Dublin Core Metadata Initiative. `http://dcevents.dublincore.org/IntConf/dc-2011/paper/view/ 52`.

EBSCO. 2015. "EBSCO Information Services." `http://www.ebsco.com`.

EDItEUR. 2009. "ONIX and MARC 21." `http://www.editeur.org/96/ONIX-and- MARC21/`.

Europeana. 2014. "The Europeana Data Model for Cultural Heritage." `http://pro. europeana.eu/c/document_library/get_file?uuid=ef2baffc-f078-41d9- be5f-76a3427f198f%5C&groupId=51031`.

FAST. 2014a. "FAST (Faceted Application of Subject Terminology) – Dataset." OCLC Research. `http://www.oclc.org/research/activities/fast/download.html`.

———. 2014b. "FAST Linked Data: FAST Authority File." OCLC Experimental. `http:// experimental.worldcat.org/fast/`.

FIU. 2014. "FIU Catalogers' Values." Libraries - Florida International University. https://library.fiu.edu/about-us/cataloging/fiu-catalogers-values.

Fons, Ted. 2013. "The Power of Shared Data." OCLCVideo on YouTube, 5 December. https://www.youtube.com/watch?v=roQ5eqAkEcE%5C&list=PLWXaAShGazu6UUnbQGs531XqVoLzDVfhM%5C&index=1.

———. 2015. "OCLC and LC Collaboration." Presentation at the BIBFRAME Update Forum, Midwinter meeting of the American Library Association, Chicago, Illinois, USA, February 1. http://www.loc.gov/bibframe/news/bibframe-update-mw2015.html.

Fons, Ted, Jeff Penka, and Richard Wallis. 2012. "OCLC's Linked Data Initiative: Using Schema.org to Make Library Data Relevant on the Web." *Information Standards Quarterly* 24 (2/3): 29–33. doi:10.3789/isqv24n2-3.2012.05.

Ford, Kevin M. 2010. "Linked Data at the Library of Congress." Presentation at SACO-At-Large, Annual Conference of the American Library Association, Washington, DC, USA, 27 June. http://id.loc.gov/about/presentations.html.

———. 2012. "LC's Bibliographic Framework Initiative and the Attractiveness of Linked Data." *Information Standards Quarterly, Special Issue: Linked Data in Libraries, Archives, and Museums* 24 (2/3). http://www.niso.org/apps/group_public/download.php/9405/SP_Ford_LC_isqv24no2-3.pdf.

Gatenby, Janifer. 2013. "Multilingual WorldCat." Presentation at the IFLA World Library and Congress: 79th IFLA General Conference and Assembly, Singapore, 19 August. http://www.oclc.org/content/dam/oclc/events/2013/IFLA2013/IFLA_Multilingual%20Presentation%202013-08-19.pdf.

Gatenby, Janifer, Richard O. Greene, W. Michael Oskins, and Gail Thornburg. 2012. "GLIMIR: Manifestation and Content Clustering within WorldCat." *The Code4Lib Journal* (17). http://journal.code4lib.org/articles/6812.

Genz, Marcella. 2002. "*The Nature of A Work: Implications for the Organization of Knowledge* by Richard P. Smiraglia." *Journal of Education for Library and Information Science* 43 (1): 87–89.

GMET. 2014. "GEneral Multilingual Environmental Thesaurus." Downloadable dataset. http://datahub.io/dataset/gemet.

GN. 2014. "GeoNames." http://www.geonames.org/.

Godby, Carol Jean. 2010. "From Records to Streams: Merging Library and Publisher Metadata." In *DC-2010: Proceedings of the International Conference on Dublin Core and Metadata Applications*, edited by Diane I. Hillman and Michael Lauruhn, 138–149. Pittsburgh, Pennsylvania, USA. Dublin Core Metadata Initiative. http://dcpapers.dublincore.org/pubs/article/view/974.

———. 2013. "The Relationship between BIBFRAME and OCLC's Linked-Data Model of Bibliographic Description: A Working Paper." http://oclc.org/content/dam/research/publications/library/2013/2013-05.pdf.

Godby, Carol Jean, and Ray Denenberg. 2015. "Common Ground: Exploring Compatibilities between the Linked Data Models of the Library of Congress and OCLC." OCLC Research. http://www.oclc.org/content/dam/research/publications/2015/oclcresearch-loc-linked-data-2015.pdf.

Godby, Carol Jean, Patricia Hswe, Larry Jackson, Judith Klavans, Lev Ratinov, and Dan Roth. 2010. "Who's Who in Your Digital Collection: Developing a Tool for Name Disambiguation and Identity Resolution." *Journal of the Chicago Colloquium on Digital Humanities and Computer Science* 1 (2). https://letterpress.uchicago.edu/index.php/jdhcs/article/view/58.

Google. 2012. "Introducing the Knowledge Graph: Things, Not Strings." In *Google Official Blog*, 16 May. http://googleblog.blogspot.com/2012/05/introducing-knowledge-graph-things-not.html.

———. 2015. "Freebase: A Community-Curated Database of People, Places, and Things." https://www.freebase.com/.

Guha, R.V. 2014. "What a Long, Strange Trip It's Been." Presentation at the 2014 Semantic Technology and Business (SemTech) Conference, San Jose, California, USA, 20 August. http://www.slideshare.net/rvguha/sem-tech2014c.

———. 2015. "Proposal for Schema.org Extension Mechanism." In *public-vocabs* [listserv], 13 February. World Wide Web Consortium.

Guha, R.V., and Dan Brickley, eds. 2014. "WebSchemas." Wiki, World Wide Web Consortium. Last modified 23 September. http://www.w3.org/wiki/WebSchemas.

Harper, Corey. 2006. "Encoding Library of Congress Subject Headings in SKOS: Authority Control for the Semantic Web." In *DC-2006: Metadata for Knowledge and Learning. Proceedings of the International Conference on Dublin Core and Metadata Applications*. Manzanillo, Comila, Mexico. Dublin Core Metadata Initiative. http://dcpapers.dublincore.org/pubs/article/view/842.

Hearst, Marti A. 1999. "Untangling Text Data Mining." In *Proceedings of the 37th Annual Meeting of the Association for Computational Linguistics on Computational Linguistics,* 3–10. College Park, Maryland, USA. doi:10.3115/1034678.1034679.

Heath, Tom, and Christian Bizer. 2011. *Linked Data: Evolving the Web into a Global Data Space.* 1–136. Synthesis Lectures on the Semantic Web: Theory and Technology, 1:1. Morgan & Claypool. doi:10.2200/S00334ED1V01Y201102WBE001.

Hepp, Martin. 2014. "GoodRelations: The Web Vocabulary for E-Commerce." http://www.heppnetz.de/projects/goodrelations/.

Herman, Ivan, Ben Adida, and Manu Sporny, eds. 2013. "RDFa 1.1 Primer - Second Edition: Rich Structured Data for Markup of Web Documents." W3C Working Group Note 22. World Wide Web Consortium. http://www.w3.org/TR/xhtml-rdfa-primer/.

Hickey, Thomas B. 2009. "The Virtual International Authority File." Presentation at the 25th Anniversary Authority Control Interest Group (ACIG) Program, Annual Conference of the American Library Association, Anaheim, California, USA, 12 July.

———. 2013. "Cooperative Authority Control: The Virtual International Authority File (VIAF)." NISO/DCMI Webinar, 4 December. http://www.slideshare.net/BaltimoreNISO/nisodcmi-webinar-cooperative-authority-control-the-virtual-international-authority-file-viaf.

Hickey, Thomas B., Edward T. O'Neill, and Jenny Toves. 2002. "Experiments with the IFLA Functional Requirements for Bibliographic Records." *D-Lib Magazine* 8 (9). http://www.dlib.org/dlib/september02/hickey/09hickey.html.

Hickey, Thomas B., and Jenny Toves. 2009. "FRBR Work-Set Algorithm Version 2.0." OCLC Research. http://www.oclc.org/content/dam/research/activities/frbralgorithm/2009-08.pdf?urlm=161376.

Hillmann, Diane, Karen Coyle, Jon Phipps, and Gordon Dunsire. 2002. "RDA Vocabularies: Process, Outcome, Use." *D-Lib Magazine* 16 (1/2). http://dlib.org/dlib/january10/hillmann/01hillmann.html.

Hodson, Tim, Corine Deliot, Alan Danskin, Heather Rosie, and Jan Ashton. 2012. "British Library Data Model – Book, V.1." West Yorkshire, United Kingdom: The British Library, 4 August. http://www.bl.uk/bibliographic/pdfs/bldatamodelbook.pdf.

IFLA. 2014. "FRBR Review Group: Frequently Asked Questions." http://www.ifla.org/node/949.

IFLA-SG. 1998. *Functional Requirements for Bibliographic Records: Final Report.* Technical report. IFLA Study Group on the Functional Requirements for Bibliographic Records. UBCIM Publications-New Series. Vol. 19. Muenchen, Germany.

Illien, Gildas. 2013. "Interview with Gildas Illien, Director, Bibliographic and Digital Information Department, Bibliothèque nationale de France (BnF)." *International Standards Quarterly* 25 (4): 22–29. doi:10.3789/isqv25no4.2013.05.

IMLS. 2015. "Institute of Museum and Library Services." http://www.imls.gov/.

Isaac, Antoine, Lourens van der Meij, Stefan Schlobach, and Shenghui Wang. 2007. "An Empirical Study of Instance-Based Ontology Matching." In *Proceedings of the 6th International Semantic Web Conference and 2nd Asian Semantic Web Conference,* 253–266. Busan, Korea. doi:10.1007/978-3-540-76298-0_19.

Isaac, Antoine, William Waites, Jeff Young, and Marcia Zeng. 2011. "Library Linked Data Incubator Group: Datasets, Value Vocabularies, and Metadata Element Sets." W3C Incubator Group Report, 25 October. World Wide Web Consortium. http://www.w3.org/2005/Incubator/lld/XGR-lld-vocabdataset-20111025/.

ISNI. 2014. "ISNI Registration Agencies." International Standard Name Identifier. http://www.isni.org/content/isni-registration-agencies.

Klein, Maximilian. 2013. "The Ropebridges: Authority Control in Wikidata." In *Hangingtogether.org* [blog], 9 May. OCLC Research. http://hangingtogether.org/?p=2878.

Klein, Maximilian, and Alex Kyrios. 2013. "VIAFbot and the Integration of Library Data on Wikipedia." *The Code4Lib Journal* (22). http://journal.code4lib.org/articles/8964.

Klyne, Graham, and Jeremy J. Carroll. 2004. "Resource Description Framework (RDF): Concepts and Abstract Syntax." W3C Recommendation, 10 February. World Wide Web Consortium. Last modified 25 February. http://www.w3.org/TR/2004/REC-rdf-concepts-20040210/.

Koopman, Rob, and Shenghui Wang. 2014. "Where Should I Publish? Detecting Journal Similarity Based on What Has Been Published There." In *Proceedings of Digital Libraries 2014,* 483–484. London, United Kingdom. Association for Computing Machinery.

Kroeger, Angela. 2013. "The Road to BIBFRAME: The Evolution of the Idea of Bibliographic Transition into a Post-MARC Future." *Cataloging & Classification Quarterly* 51 (8): 873–890. doi:10.1080/01639374.2013.823584.

Landry, Patrice. 2009. "Multilingualism and Subject Heading Languages: How the MACS Project Will be Providing Multilingual Subject Access in Europe." *Catalogue & Index* (157): 9–11.

LC. 2000. "MARC21 Format for Holdings Data. 2000 Edition." Network Development and MARC Standards Office. Library of Congress. http://www.loc.gov/marc/holdings/echdhome.html.

———. 2008a. "MARC to Dublin Core Crosswalk." Development and MARC Standards Office. Library of Congress. http://www.loc.gov/marc/marc2dc.html.

———. 2008b. "On the Record: Report of the Library of Congress Working Group on the Future of Bibliographic Control." Library of Congress. Last modified 9 January. http://www.loc.gov/bibliographic-future/news/lcwg-ontherecord-jan08-final.pdf.

———. 2012. "MADS RDF Primer." Library of Congress. Last modified 10 May. http://www.loc.gov/standards/mads/rdf/.

———. 2014a. "240 - Uniform Title (NR)." In *MARC 21 Format for Bibliographic Data. 1999 Edition.* Network Development and MARC Standards Office. Library of Congress. http://www.loc.gov/marc/bibliographic/bd130.html.

———. 2014b. "BIBFRAME: Bibliographic Framework Initiative." Library of Congress. http://www.loc.gov/bibframe/.

———. 2014c. "BIBFRAME Model and Vocabulary." Library of Congress. http://www.loc.gov/bibframe/docs/.

———. 2014d. "MARC 21 Format for Authority Data. 1999 Edition." Network Development and MARC Standards Office. Library of Congress. Last modified 20 October. http://www.loc.gov/marc/authority/ecadhome.html.

———. 2014e. "MARC 21 Format for Bibliographic Data. 1999 Edition." Network Development and MARC Standards Office. Library of Congress. http://www.loc.gov/marc/bibliographic/ecbdhome.html.

———. 2014f. "Metadata Object Description Schema (MODS): MARC 21 to MODS 3.5 Mapping." Library of Congress. Revised October 2014. http://www.loc.gov/standards/mods/mods-mapping.html.

———. 2015. "BIBFRAME Implementation Testbed." Library of Congress. http://www.oclc.org/content/dam/research/publications/2015/oclcresearch-loc-linked-data-2015.pdf.

LD4L. 2015a. "Breakout: Entity Resolution(Strings to Things)." LD4L Workshop, Stanford University, Palo Alto, California, USA, 23 February. https://wiki.duraspace.org/pages/viewpage.action?pageId=68062627.

———. 2015b. "Linked Data for Libraries (LD4L)." DuraSpace wiki. Last modified 6 February. https://wiki.duraspace.org/pages/viewpage.action?pageId=413540281.

Lenant, Douglas, and R.V. Guha. 1989. *Building Large Knowledge-Based Systems: Representation and Inference in the Cyc Project.* Boston, Massachusetts, USA: Addison Wesley-Longman Publishing Co.

MB. 2015. "MusicBrainz." MetaBrainz Foundation. Last modified 23 February. https://musicbrainz.org/.

McCallum, Sally. 2015. "BIBFRAME Update." Presentation at the OCLC *Collective Insight* series *Library Data [R]evolution: Applying Linked Data Concepts*, Palo Alto, California, USA, 25 February. OCLCVideo on YouTube. https://www.youtube.com/watch?v=GJsoV7zidAw%5C&list=PLWXaAShGazu6UUnbQGs531XqVoLzDVfhM%5C&index=2.

Miles, Alistair, and Sean Bechhofer. 2009a. "SKOS Simple Knowledge Organization System eXtension for Labels: (SKOS-XL) Namespace Document - HTML Variant." 18th August 2009 Recommendation Edition. World Wide Web Consortium. http://www.w3.org/TR/skos-reference/skos-xl.html.

———. 2009b. "SKOS Simple Knowledge Organization System: Reference." W3C Recommendation, 18 August. World Wide Web Consortium. http://www.w3.org/TR/2009/REC-skos-reference-20090818/.

———. 2009c. "SKOS Simple Knowledge Organization System: The SKOS: Concept Class." *SKOS Simple Knowledge Organization System Reference.* W3C Recommendation, 18 August. World Wide Web Consortium. http://www.w3.org/TR/2009/REC-skos-reference-20090818/#concepts.

Miller, Eric. 2014. "Libhub: Leading, Learning, and Linking." Zepheira. http://www.libhub.org.

Miller, Eric, and Bob Schloss, eds. 1997. "Resource Description Framework (RDF) Model and Syntax." Version 1, 2 October. World Wide Web Consortium. http://www.w3.org/TR/WD-rdf-syntax-971002/.

Mitchell, Joan, and Michael Panzer. 2013. "Dewey Linked Data: Making Connections with Old Friends and New Acquaintances." *Italian Journal of Library and Information Science* 4 (1): 177–199. http://leo.cineca.it/index.php/jlis/article/view/5467.

Mixter, Jeffrey K., and Eric Childress. 2013. "FAST (Faceted Application of Subject Terminology) Users: Summary and Case Studies." OCLC Research. http://www.oclc.org/content/dam/research/publications/library/2013/2013-04.pdf.

Mixter, Jeffrey K., Patrick OBrien, and Kenning Arlitsch. 2014. "Describing Theses and Dissertations Using Schema.org." In *DC-2014: Proceedings of the International Conference on Dublin Core and Metadata Applications.* Austin, Texas, USA. Dublin Core Metadata Initiative. http://dcpapers.dublincore.org/pubs/article/download/3715/1938.

Nelson, Theodor H. 1974. *Computer Lib: You Can and Must Understand Computers Now.* Chicago, Illinois, USA: Nelson.

OCLC. 1998. "xISBN Bookmarklet and Library Lookup service (V2)." OCLC WorldCat Service. http://xissn.worldcat.org/liblook2/index.htm.

———. 2011a. "FAST Converter: Convert LCSH Subject Headings to FAST Subject Headings." OCLC Experimental, a project of OCLC Research. Last modified 5 May. http://oclc.org/research/activities/fastconverter.html.

———. 2011b. "OCLC Releases FAST (Faceted Application of Subject Terminology) as Linked Data." OCLC news release, 14 December. http://www.oclc.org/news/releases/2011/201171.en.html.

———. 2012. "OCLC Adds Linked Data to WorldCat.org." OCLC news release, 20 June. http://www.oclc.org/news/releases/2012/201238.en.html.

———. 2014a. "2014 Annual Report to VIAF Council." http://oclc.org/content/dam/oclc/viaf/OCLC-2014-VIAF-Annual-Report-to-VIAF-Council.pdf.

———. 2014b. "Learn More about WorldCat Works." OCLC Developer Network, 29 April. https://www.oclc.org/developer/news/2014/learn-more-about-worldcat-works.en.html.

———. 2014c. "Linked Data Survey." Excel spreadsheet, OCLC Research. http://oclc.org/research/activities/linkeddata.html#linked-data-surveyl.

———. 2014d. "OCLC Releases WorldCat Works as Linked Data." OCLC news release, 28 April. https://www.oclc.org/news/releases/2014/201414dublin.en.html.

———. 2014e. "The WorldCat Digital Collection Gateway." http://www.oclc.org/digital-gateway.en.html.

OMR. 2014. "Open Metadata Registry: Supporting Metadata Interoperability." Open Metadata Registry. http://metadataregistry.org/.

O'Neill, Edward T. 2002. "FRBR: Application of the Entity-Relationship Model to Humphry Clinker." *Library Resources & Technical Services* 46 (4): 150–159.

———. 2014. "FAST: Subject Headings for the Semantic Web." Presentation at the Midwinter Meeting of the American Library Association, Philadelphia, Pennsylvania, USA, 28 January. http://connect.ala.org/node/217667.

ORCID. 2015. "ORCID: Connecting Research and Researchers." Last modified 27 January. http://orcid.org.

Panzer, Michael. 2008. "DDC, SKOS, and Linked Data on the Web." Presentation at the OCLC/ISKO-NA Preconference, Montreal, Canada, 5 August. http://slideplayer.us/slide/723100/.

———. 2012. "From Strings to Things: Cataloging & Linked Data." Presentation at the RBMS (Rare Books and Manuscripts) preconference "Futures." San Diego, California, USA, 21 June. http://www.slideshare.net/mobile/mapanzer/from-strings-to-things-cataloging-linked-data.

Panzer, Michael, and Marcia Zeng. 2009. "Modeling Classification Systems in SKOS: Some Challenges and Best-Practice Recommendations." In *DC-2009: Proceedings of the International Conference on Dublin Core and Metadata Applications.* Seoul, South Korea. Dublin Core Metadata Initiative. http://dcpapers.dublincore.org/pubs/article/view/974.

Pattuelli, M. Cristina, Matt Miller, Leanora Lange, Sean Fitzell, and Carolyn Li Madeo. 2013. "Crafting Linked Open Data for Cultural Heritage: Mapping and Curation Tools for the Linked Jazz Project." *The Code4Lib Journal* (21). http://journal.code4lib.org/articles/8670.

PSU. 2014. "CiteSeer." College of Information Sciences and Technology, Pennsylvania State University. http://citeseerx.ist.psu.edu/index;jsessionid=CF5ED1EE927E84F4FC08BEE4FB3C01EC.

PTO. 2015. "The Product Types Ontology: High-Precision Identifiers for Product Types Based on Wikipedia." Product Types Ontology. Last modified 2 February. http://www.productontology.org/.

PU. 2013. "WordNet: a Lexical Database for English." Last modified 26 August. Princeton University. http://wordnet.princeton.edu/.

Raman, T.V., ed. 2006. "On Linking Alternative Representations to Enable Discovery and Publishing." TAG Finding, 1 November. World Wide Web Consortium. http://www.w3.org/2001/tag/doc/alternatives-discovery.html.

RDA. 2010. "RDA Toolkit: Resource Description and Access." http://www.rdatoolkit.org/.

Rekkavik, Asgeir. 2014. "RDF Linked Data Cataloguing at Oslo Public Library." *SCATnews: Newsletter of the Standing Committee of the IFLA Cataloguing Section* 41:13–16. http://www.ifla.org/files/assets/cataloguing/scatn/scat-news-41.pdf.

Ridge, Mia. 2012. "From 'Strings to Things'." Keynote presentation at the LODLAM Melbourne workshop, Melbourne, Australia, 17 April. http://www.miaridge.com/keynote-from-strings-to-things-lodlam-melbourne-workshop/.

Ronallo, Jason. 2012. "HTML 5 Microdata and Schema.org." *The Code4lib Journal* (16). http://journal.code4lib.org/articles/6400.

———. 2013. "Schema.org Documentation Should Show Multiple Inheritance Chains When Multiple Parents for Type." In *public-vocabs* [listserv], 26 January. World Wide Web Consortium. http://lists.w3.org/Archives/Public/public-vocabs/2013Jan/0140.html.

Sauermann, Leo, and Richard Cyganiac. 2007. "Cool URIs for the Semantic Web." W3C Interest Group Note, 3 December. World Wide Web Consortium. http://www.w3.org/TR/cooluris/.

Schema. 2012. "Schema.org Core Schema." http://schema.org/docs/schema_org_rdfa.html.

Schema Bib Extend. 2014a. "Collection." W3C Community and Business Groups. World Wide Web Consortium. http://www.w3.org/community/schemabibex/wiki/Collection.

———. 2014b. "Holdings via Offer." W3C Community and Business Groups. World Wide Web Consortium. http://www.w3.org/community/schemabibex/wiki/Holdings_via_Offer.

———. 2014c. "Recipes and Guidelines." W3C Community and Business Groups. World Wide Web Consortium. http://www.w3.org/community/schemabibex/wiki/Recipes_and_Guidelines.

———. 2014d. "Schema Bib Extend Community Group." W3C Community and Business Groups. World Wide Web Consortium. http://www.w3.org/community/schemabibex/.

Schema.org. 2014a. "Thing–>Product." http://schema.org/Product.

———. 2014b. "Thing–>Product–>IndividualProduct." http://schema.org/IndividualProduct.

Schema.org. 2014c. "Thing–>Property–>workExample." http://schema.org/workExample.

Scott, Dan. 2014. "RDFa + Schema.org." Preconference workshop at the Annual Meeting of the American Library Association, Las Vegas, Nevada, USA, 27 June. http://stuff.coffeecode.net/2014/lld_preconference/.

Shvaiko, Pavel, and Jerome Euzenat. 2013. "Ontology Matching: State of the Art and Future Challenges." *IEEE Transactions on Knowledge and Data Engineering* 25 (1): 158–176. doi:10.1109/TKDE.2011.253.

Simon, Agnes, Romain Wenz, Vincent Michel, and Adrien Mascio. 2013. "Publishing Bibliographic Records on the Web of Data: Opportunities for the BnF (French National Library)." In *The Semantic Web: Semantics and Big Data*, edited by Philipp Cimiano, Oscar Corcho, Valentina Presutti, Laura Hollink, and Sebastian Rudolph, 7882:563–577. Lecture Notes in Computer Science. Berlin, Germany: Springer. doi:10.1007/978-3-642-38288-8_38.

Smiralgia, Richard P., ed. 2001. *The Nature of a Work: Implications for the Organization of Knowledge.* Lanham, Maryland, USA: Scarecrow Press.

Smith-Yoshimura, Karen. 2013. "First Scholars' Contributions to VIAF: Greek!" In *Hangingtogether.org* [blog], 25 November. OCLC Research. http://hangingtogether.org/?p=3455.

———. 2014a. "Linked Data Survey Results 3: Why and What Institutions are Consuming." In *Hangingtogether.org* [blog], 1 September. OCLC Research. http://hangingtogether.org/?p=4155.

———. 2014b. "Multilingual Bibliographic Structure." OCLC Research Update at ALA Annual Conference. http://www.slideshare.net/oclcr/oclc-research-update-ala-annual-2014.

Smith-Yoshimura, Karen, Micah Altman, Michael Conlon, Ana Lupe Cristan, Laura Dawson, Joanne Dunham, Thom Hickey, et al. 2014. "Registering Researchers in Authority Files." OCLC Research. http://www.oclc.org/content/dam/research/publications/library/2014/oclcresearchregistering-researchers-2014-a4.pdf.

Smith-Yoshimura, Karen, Catherine Argus, Timothy J. Dickey, Chew Chiat Naun, Lisa Rowlinson de Ortiz, and Hugh Taylor. 2010. "Implications of MARC Tag Usage on Library Metadata Practices." Report produced by OCLC Research in support of the RLG Partnership. http://www.oclc.org/research/publications/library/2010/2010-06.pdf.

Smith-Yoshimura, Karen, and David Michelson. 2013. "Irreconcilable Differences? Name Authority Control & Humanities Scholarship." In *Hangingtogether.org* [blog], 27 March. OCLC Research. http://hangingtogether.org/?p=2621.

Stolz, Alex. 2014. "RDF Translator, Powered by RDFLib 4.0.1." Universitaet der Bundeswehr Muenchen. http://rdf-translator.appspot.com/.

Summers, Ed, Antoine Isaac, Clay Redding, and Dan Krech. 2008. "LCSH, SKOS, and Linked Data." In *DC-2008: Proceedings of the International Conference on Dublin Core and Metadata Applications*, 25–33. Berlin, Germany. Dublin Core Metadata Initiative. http://edoc.hu-berlin.de/conferences/dc-2008/summers-ed-25/PDF/summers.pdf.

TEL. 2014a. "The BNF Transforms the Visibility of its Resources with Linked Open Data." In *The European Library. Connecting Knowledge. About Us / News Item*, 14 May. The European Library. http://www.theeuropeanlibrary.org/tel4/newsitem/5350.

———. 2014b. "The European Library." http://www.theeuropeanlibrary.org/tel4/.

Tillett, Barbara. 2003. "The FRBR Model (Functional Requirements for Bibliographic Records)." Presentation to the ALCTS Institute on Metadata and AACR2, San Jose, California, USA, 4-5 April. http://www.loc.gov/catdir/cpso/frbreng.pdf.

———. 2004. "What is FRBR? A Conceptual Model Model for the Bibliographic Universe." Library of Congress Cataloging Distribution Service. http://www.loc.gov/cds/downloads/FRBR.PDF.

URI-PIG. 2001. "URIs, URLs, and URNs: Clarifications and Recommendations 1." W3C Note, 21 September. URI Planning Interest Group. World Wide Web Consortium and Internet Engineering Task Force. http://www.w3.org/TR/uri-clarification/.

VIAF. 2014. "The Virtual International Authority File." http://viaf.org/.

Vizine-Goetz, Diane. 2013. "WorldCat Cookbook Finder: Explore Cookbooks and More from Libraries around the World." OCLC Research. http://oclc.org/research/activities/cookbook-finder.html.

———. 2014a. "Classify: An Experimental Classification Web Service." OCLC Research. http://www.oclc.org/research/activities/classify.html.

———. 2014b. "Kindred Works: A Demonstration Interface for an Experimental World-Cat Recommender Service." OCLC Research. http://www.oclc.org/research/activities/kindredworks.html.

W3C-OWL. 2012. "OWL 2 Web Ontology Language: Document Overview (Second Edition)." W3C Recommendation, 11 December. W3C OWL Working Group. World Wide Web Consortium. http://www.w3.org/TR/2012/REC-owl2-overview-20121211/.

Wallis, Richard. 2013. "What the Web Wants." OCLCVideo on YouTube, 6 December. https : / / www . youtube . com / watch ? v = GJsoV7zidAw % 5C & list = PLWXaAShGazu6UUnbQGs531XqVoLzDVfhM%5C&index=2.

———. 2014a. "A Step for Schema.org – A Leap for Bib Data on the Web." In *Data Liberate* [blog], 2 September. http://dataliberate.com/2014/09/a-step-for-schema-org-a-leap-for-bib-data-on-the-web/.

———. 2014b. "WorldCat Works Linked Data – Some Answers to Early Questions." In *Data Liberate* [blog], 4 March. http : / / dataliberate . com / 2014 / 03 / worldcat - works - linked-data-some-answers-to-early-questions/.

Wallis, Richard, and Dan Cohen. 2014. "Schema.org Support for Bibiographic Relationships and Periodicals." In *Schema blog: Official blog for schema.org*, 2 September. http : / / blog . schema . org/2014/09/schemaorg-support-for-bibliographic_2.html.

Wang, Shenghui, Gwenn Englebienne, and Stefan Schlobach. 2008. "Learning Concept Mappings from Instance Similarity." In *Proceedings of the 7th International Semantic Web Conference*, 339–355. Karlsruhe, Germany. doi:10.1007/978-3-540-88564-1_22.

Wang, Shenghui, Antoine Isaac, Valentine Charles, Rob Koopman, Anti Agoropoulou, and Titia van der Werf. 2013. "Hierarchical Structuring of Cultural Heritage Objects within Large Aggregations." In *Proceedings of 17th International Conference on Theory and Practice of Digital Libraries*, 247–259. Valletta, Malta. doi:10.1007/978-3-642-40501-3_25.

Wang, Shenghui, Antoine Isaac, Stefan Schlobach, Lourens van der Meij, and Balthasar A. C. Schopman. 2012. "Instance-based Semantic Interoperability in the Cultural Heritage." *Semantic Web* 3 (1): 45–64. doi:10.3233/SW-2012-0045.

Wang, Shenghui, Antoine Isaac, Balthasar A. C. Schopman, Stefan Schlobach, and Lourens van der Meij. 2009. "Matching Multi-lingual Subject Vocabularies." In *Proceedings of the 13th European Conference on Digital Libraries*, 125–137. Corfu, Greece. doi:10.1007/978-3-642-04346-8_14.

Weibel, Stuart, Jean Godby, Eric Miller, and Ron Daniel. 1995. "OCLC/NCSA Metadata Workshop Report." Metadata Innovation. Dublin Core Metadata Initiative. http : / / dublincore.org/workshops/dc1/report.shtml.

Will, Leonard. 2001. "Costs of Vocabulary Mapping." Presentation at High-level Thesaurus (HILT) workshop. http : / / www . authorstream . com / Presentation / Jade - 31848 - Leonard-Costs-vocabulary-mapping-Different-kinds-subject-vocabularies-Ways-Input-output-via-re-will-as-Entertainment-ppt-powerpoint/.

WWW. 1991. "World Wide Web." http://info.cern.ch/hypertext/WWW/TheProject.html.

Yee, Martha M. 2009. "Can Bibliographic Data be Put Directly on the Semantic Web?" Boston College University Libraries. http://ejournals.bc.edu/ojs/index.php/ital/article/download/3175/2788.

Young, Jeff. 2011. "Changes to VIAF's RDF." In *Outgoing* [blog], 12 April. http://outgoing.typepad.com/outgoing/2011/04/.

Zeng, Marcia Lei, Maja Zumer, and Athena Salaba, eds. 2010. *Functional Requirements for Subject Authority Data (FRSAD): A Conceptual Model.* Technical report. IFLA Working Group on the Functional Requirements for Subject Authority Records (FRSAR). http://www.ifla.org/files/assets/classification-and-indexing/functional-requirements-for-subject-authority-data/frsad-final-report.pdf.

Zumer, Maja, Edward T. O'Neill, and Jeffrey K. Mixter. 2015. "FRBR Aggregates: Their Types and Frequency in LIbrary Collections." To appear in July, *Library Resources and Technical Services* 59 (3).

Authors' Biographies

CAROL JEAN GODBY

Carol Jean Godby is a Senior Research Scientist at OCLC, where she has directed projects with a focus on automated content analysis that produce research prototypes, open source software, improvements to national and international standards, and enhancements to OCLC's products, services, and data architecture. She has a Ph.D. in linguistics from Ohio State University. Her work on mapping library standards for bibliographic description is widely known to librarians and publishers. Since 2012, she has been a leader of a cross-division team at OCLC whose charter is to develop a next-generation data architecture based on the principles of linked data.

SHENGHUI WANG

Shenghui Wang is a Research Scientist at the OCLC EMEA office in Leiden, The Netherlands. Her current research activities include text and data mining as well as Linked Data investigations. She received a Ph.D. in Computer Science from the University of Manchester in 2007. Shenghui has been conducting research in the broad field of Artificial Intelligence with interests in cognitive modeling, knowledge representation and reasoning, natural language semantics, and machine learning. Before joining OCLC Research in 2012, Shenghui was a researcher at the Free University of Amsterdam and Wageningen University, exploring Semantic Web and language technologies to improve the semantic interoperability in the domain of cultural heritage and agrifood research.

JEFFREY K. MIXTER

Jeffrey K. Mixter is a recent graduate of Kent State University, having earned an M.L.I.S. (Masters of Library and Information Science) and an M.S. degree in Information Architecture and Knowledge Management. His master's thesis demonstrated how to convert an existing flat data model into a detailed ontology that is interoperable with search engine aggregating services. As a Research Assistant at OCLC, Jeff worked with Dr. Ed O'Neill in developing the OCLC FAST controlled vocabulary. He is now working as a Software Engineer at OCLC with collaborators from Montana State University on the IMLS-funded project 'Measuring Up: Assessing Accuracy of Reported Use and Impact of Digital Repositories.' Kenning Arlitsch, Dean of Libraries at Montana State, is the principal investigator. Jeff's role in the project is to serve as a data modeling expert, taking the lead in the development of an ontology for modeling items found in institutional repositories and digital collections in a form that can be discovered and indexed by Google and other major search engines.

CPSIA information can be obtained at www.ICGtesting.com
Printed in the USA
LVOW01s2355230615

443578LV00001B/1/P